QUANTITATIVE APPROA
IN BUSINESS STUDIES

Fourth edition

Lecturer's Guide

CLARE MORRIS

PITMAN
PUBLISHING

London · Hong Kong · Johannesburg · Melbourne · Singapore · Washington DC

PITMAN PUBLISHING
128 Long Acre, London WC2 9AN
Tel: +44 (0)171 447 2000
Fax: +44 (0)171 240 5771

A Division of Pearson Professional Limited

First Published in Great Britain 1993
Fourth edition

ISBN 0 273 62329 X

British Library Cataloguing in Publication Data
A CIP catalogue record for this book can be obtained from the British Library

Typeset by Avocet Typeset, Brill, Aylesbury, Bucks
Printed and bound in Great Britain

The Publishers' policy is to use paper manufactured from sustainable forests

Contents

Notes to the reader

Objectives of this guide

This lecturer's guide aims to provide:

- a summary of the key aspects of each chapter's of the book;
- some personal reflections on the teaching of each chapter's material;
- full solutions to the numerical exercises, and suggestions for tackling the non-numerical ones;
- some further suggestions for practical/experimental work.

Introduction

I feel extremely diffident about writing a Lecturer's Guide to accompany *Quantitative Approaches in Business Studies* since the secret of good teaching is surely to make the material one's own, and to teach from a basis of conviction and experience. To attempt to follow someone else's style is almost certainly to court problems – not to mention the fact that the treatment of a topic such as, for instance, correlation will change significantly depending on whether it is being taught to an HND Business Studies group, a class studying for a professional accounting qualification, or an MBA group.

In what follows, therefore, I will not presume to do more than suggest possible ways in which the material of the book may be utilised, and to mention some aspects of my own experience in teaching this material which may possibly be of interest to colleagues. One of the features which characterises our subject area is the scope for differences of opinion, even on apparently simple matters such as specification of class limits in frequency tables. Students, of course, nearly always exhibit a strong desire to be 'told how to do it' – in other words, they do not like to have to cope with divergences of opinion, or with the need to make choices about methods. I regard it as perhaps my primary objective, in teaching quantitative methods at a Higher Education level, to confront students whenever possible with a diversity of possible approaches, and to a large extent to eschew 'right answers' – even, the reader may feel, to the point of vagueness at times. So, if somewhere along the line in this Guide, I manage to offend against your favourite prejudice, or to omit your favourite teaching point, I will regard that as a positive strength!

Assumed readership of the book

Quantitative Approaches in Business Studies was originally designed for use with HNC/D and first year degree students on Business Studies courses, with a secondary objective of catering for the needs of those studying for professional qualifications such as IPD and CIMA. Since the first edition appeared in 1983, however, the book has found favour for use with other courses, including MBAs.

In spite of the apparent variety of level among these different groups of users, I think we can identify certain common features, leading in turn to common challenges in teaching such students.

1 A wide variety of background, ranging from students with A level or perhaps even degree level qualifications in mathematics/statistics, to those with a poor performance in GCSE/O level/CSE, often achieved several years ago. This means that we, as teachers, need to offer a stimulating and stretching experience to the more able, while trying not to alarm or demotivate the nervous!

2 An interest in the subject (if any) which is strongly based on its perceived usefulness for management applications rather than its intrinsic value. Thus, immediately concepts are introduced, they must be justified on practical grounds – and students' perceptions of 'relevance' are often distressingly narrow, even when they have plenty of business experience.

3 Consequent on point (2), a lack of interest in formal proofs of results. The positive aspect of this is that there is often a strong instinct to apply 'common-sense' criteria to the statements of a lecturer or text – this is an instinct which should be exploited as often as possible.

It seems to me that these characteristics suggest that the only approach which is going to be really successful with such groups of students is a strongly problem-focused one, presupposing a very small amount of mathematical knowledge and facility.

However, if the emphasis moves too much towards 'real' problems, with all that it implies – 'messy' data in large quantities, multiple objectives, etc. – there is a danger that our customers will be unable to see the wood for the trees. Hence my decision, while using a problem to motivate each topic area introduced, not to make heavy use of real data. Once the student has gained confidence in a method, of course, it may well be appropriate for him or her to move on to use it in a 'real' context, and I will make some suggestions about this at various points in the Guide.

Note to the fourth edition

Major changes introduced in this edition include:

● the addition of a complete chapter (Chapter 12) on statistical applications in the field of quality improvement;

● a complete restructuring of Chapter 13 on correlation;

● a change from LOTUS 1-2-3 to EXCEL as the spreadsheet used for examples, with corresponding changes to the material on the disk;

● updating of the MINITAB material to refer to MINITAB version 10 for Windows;

● the introduction of more worked examples throughout the book;

● the provision of more exercises, solutions to which will be gound in this Guide.

All these changes were made in response to suggestions from users of the third edition.

Chapter 1
BASIC NUMERACY SKILLS

Outline content

This chapter covers all the arithmetical and algebraic requirements of subsequent chapters; conversely, nothing is included which will not be needed later in the book.

The arithmetical work covers:
- **real numbers, positive and negative;**
- **fractions and fractional operations;**
- **decimals;**
- **percentages;**
- **significant figures and rounding.**

Algebraic topics cover:
- **notation;**
- **simple linear equations and pairs of simultaneous linear equations;**
- **graph-plotting;**
- **use of algebraic methods to solve practical problems.**

Teaching this material

Students tackling the material of this chapter can be divided into three groups.

1 Those for whom it will hold no problems.

2 Those who have not thought about these methods for some years, and who may be 'rusty' and lacking in confidence. Their main need is for plenty of practice, and encouragement to develop confidence. It is also important, if possible, to ask about the methods they have used in the past, to avoid potential confusions, for example, there are several alternative methods for the solution of simultaneous equations, apart from the one given in the chapter. We need to assure students of the validity of familiar methods (assuming they are correctly recalled), and not to insist upon their mastering another unfamiliar method when they already have a perfectly adequate one under their belts.

3 The student with genuine numeracy problems. These students often have very garbled recollections of methods learned by rote at school; not understood then or now. We need to go back to square one, to explain – slowly, carefully and several times if necessary – the reasoning behind these apparently arbitrary methods, and to provide plenty of graded examples for practice. Students in this group often respond better to practically-oriented examples than to routine mathematical calculations. I have, in the past, set a question concerning the number of circular table-tops of a given diameter which can be cut from a rectangular sheet of wood. One or two of the 'more numerate' students in the group, who recalled 'advanced' topics such as the

formula for calculating the area of a circle, computed this area and divided it into the area of the sheet. It took a 'non-numerate' student to point out that you can't roll up leftover wood as if it were plasticine and cut it up again!

Personally, I would not teach the material of this chapter as a block. It can be used as preliminary course reading, with students using the initial test to determine which sections they need to study. Some topics which commonly cause confusion may need a brief recap, for example, percentages, plotting and interpretation of linear graphs, but the majority are best consolidated as and when they are required in later work.

Solutions

No solutions to the routine problems in this chapter are provided – the answers are all in the book.

Chapter 3
SAMPLING METHODS

Outline content

This chapter discusses:
- **the nature of statistical data;**
- **sources of secondary data, with some advice on using these;**
- **sampling strategies for collecting primary data;**
- **questionnaire design.**

Teaching this material

The content of this chapter, being primarily descriptive, can make for rather tedious lecture material. There is a tendency for the listener to feel that the principles involved are 'obvious', unless there is a strong back-up of practical work. Students generally have a good deal of experience in this area to draw on – most will have been 'victims' of a market research survey at some time, and there are plenty of questionnaires around these days for discussion.

One major pitfall in discussing sample design is the difference between the colloquial and statistical uses of the word 'random'. To most people, this simply means 'haphazard', so that a quota sample would look 'random' in this sense. It is vital to make clear that we are using the word in a much more specific way, otherwise a lot of confusion may ensue when moving on to discuss sampling theory.

Solutions to the exercises

1 (a) A systematic sample (every tenth person to give 10 per cent) seems most obvious here. Possible sources of bias could be discussed such as:

- would the fact that we are doing the survey on one particular day have an effect?
- are there seasonal variations to consider?
- what about people who don't or can't come in person to collect and thus will not be represented in the sample?

(b) The sample would need to be stratified by category (manual/non-manual) and by grade. For example, if the 1,500 workforce is made up of 375 non-manual workers and 1,125 manual workers, then a proportionate stratified sample of 200 would contain 50 non-manual and 150 manual workers. The selection of individual respondents could be done by using Works Numbers generated randomly.

Possible discussion points: with a sample of only 200, if there are many subgroups within the workforce, it may be difficult to reflect them all adequately in the sample. We have to trade off a well-structured sample against a reasonably small one.

The natural instinct is to go for a proportionate stratified sample, but there may be cases where the topic of the survey means we would like to have certain groups more heavily represented in the sample. Here, it might be the case that non-manual workers tend to travel farther to the location of the present factory, so they would not be so concerned about the effect of the move as manual workers. We might, therefore, structure the sample to include a more than proportionate number of manual workers.

One advantage of the stratified approach is that we can simultaneously collect information for subgroups in the population and for the population as a whole.

(c) This would be quite difficult to arrange in practice – there will be marked variations between the male/female make-up of the customers at different times of the day and week. There should be a quota of data to be collected at various times during one week (which should be 'typical', i.e. not the pre-Christmas week, for example, when more than the usual number of men will be accompanying their families).

There is also the question of what precisely is meant by a 'customer'. Do we mean the person paying the bill? If a couple are shopping together, do they count as one male and one female customer?

(d) It should be quite easy to take a genuine simple random sample in this situation, using account numbers. A systematic sample would also be a possibility unless, as seems unlikely, there is some underlying pattern to the occurrence of errors. It might be easier to program the selection of such a sample.

2 (a) Although the weight of a bag of sweets is in principle a continuous variable, it is worth discussing the way in which the accuracy of measuring equipment, and the system of rounding measurements may affect the quoted results.

(b) The number of sweets per bag is clearly a discrete variable.

(c) Stock levels would be a discrete variable. If stocks held were very large it might be desirable to treat them as effectively continuous for purposes of analysis, but it is unlikely that this would be the case with stocks of shoes held by a retailer, where relatively small numbers of a large number of lines are likely to be held.

(d) The question of stocks of grain is the reverse of that discussed in the previous example. Though these stocks will in principle be measurable by a continuous variable such as weight, or perhaps, volume, in practice they are likely to be treated in discrete units (sacks, nearest whole tonne, etc.).

3 (a) A leading question – especially if delivered verbally in tones of surprise. The question assumes that visitors do create litter and mess, and that the respondent is likely to object. A better version would split the two issues:

● Do you believe that summer visitors are responsible for increased litter in the town? (Yes/No/Not sure)
● If yes, do you object to this? (Yes/No/Not sure)

(b) This one would be very difficult for most people to answer – and the responses would be very difficult to analyse. A parameter such as class can best be assessed via indirect evidence such as occupation, for example. Moreover, there are standard definitions of social class, as related to occupation, which should be used in any extensive survey for purposes of comparability with other work.

(c) Two questions are rolled into one here. They should be split into:

- Do you believe facilities provided by the council for visitors are adequate? (Yes/No/Not sure)
- If your answer to the previous question was No, which of the following additional facilities do you think are needed? (Provide a list of possible responses including 'other – please specify'. More than one may be indicated.)

(d) Hypothetical question – there is nothing wrong with the wording of the question as such, but to ask about future intentions gives notoriously unreliable results. In this case, more people would probably indicate an interest in the pool than would actually use it, simply because they like the idea.

4 It is impossible to give 'correct' solutions to this question – the value to the student lies in discussing the possible measurement methods, and the problems which could arise.

(a) For this problem, methods could range from an extensive questionnaire following a graduate training programme, to a simple measure such as 'number of reject quality items produced' following training in carrying out a simple production process.

(b) This would almost certainly require some kind of sample survey of potential purchasers, which would have to be carefully structured to reflect the make up of the target population.

(c) The response here could again be survey-based, though in a fairly small organisation a census rather than a sample could be used. How do you define 'favourability'? – by the response to a question such as 'If this new clothing were introduced, would you wear it?' It might be possible to organise a small practical trial of the new clothing and worker response to this would provide more extensive evidence.

(d) This could be done fairly easily by classifying applicants according to highest level of academic achievement – GCSE, A Level, and so on. Even so, there are many non-standard qualifications which would need to be carefully allowed for in such a classification.

5 The answers to these questions are not in themselves of interest, but searching them out should introduce students to the wide variety of published statistical information. I have found answers to these particular questions in the *Motor Industry of Great Britain* (published by the Society of Motor Manufacturers and Traders); *Regional Trends*; the *Monthly Digest of Statistics*; the *Post Office Annual Report and Accounts*; and the *Census of Retail Premises*; but no doubt they are also available from other sources.

6 This task might be better carried out by pairs or groups of students rather than individuals.

(a) For scenario A, the term 'the general public' needs to be more carefully defined before a sample can be selected. Some kind of quota sample is probably called for, but thought needs to be given to relevant subgroups – age is likely to be one, since the type of catering which suits a group of senior citizens is unlikely to appeal to the members of a rugby club.

Under B, depending on the size of the organisation involved it may be possible to survey everyone – that is, to conduct a census rather than a sample. If a sample is required, it could be done systematically from personnel records. It is likely that those responding will be the people most interested in sporting activities – in a sense this creates bias, but if the objective of the survey is to determine the kind of facilities required, this is not really a problem.

For C, 'consumer' needs to be pinned down more closely. Again, a quota sample will be simplest, but appropriate groupings need care – ability/willingness to pay more for environmentally-friendly products may be related to parameters such as income, etc.

Sampling methods for D would be similar to those for B.

(b) Drafting the questionnaire involves not only deciding the number of questions and their wording, but also determining their order. Is the questionnaire to be administered verbally or given to respondents to complete on paper? If computer analysis of the responses is to be carried out, simple validity checks can be discussed, and issues of non-response and the handling of multiple-response questions can be raised.

(c) Before carrying out the pilot survey, it is helpful for students to exchange and constructively criticise each others' draft questionnaires.

(d) Presentation of findings can introduce topics such as pie charts, which will be encountered again in Chapter 5. Alternatively, discussion of this part of the work could be deferred until after that chapter has been covered. Students could give an oral presentation on their results, using MINITAB or Excel to produce graphics and tables.

(e) Discussion of the problems encountered, and the changes required to the pilot survey, can be the most fruitful part of the process. The major learning outcome of the exercise should be to convince students that designing a good survey, which gives the required information in the form in which you want it, is not so simple as it might seem.

Suggestions for further work

Students can be asked to collect samples of questionnaires from newspapers, etc, which can then form the basis for discussion and criticism.

Depending on the data sources available in your institution's library, further questions along the lines of Exercise 5 can be constructed to reflect student's specialist interests (in marketing, tourism, etc).

Chapter 4
DATA INTERPRETATION

Outline content

This chapter gives a brief overview of the problem of 'eyeballing' data, and discusses methods for the rough checking of figures.

Teaching this material

The material which this chapter attempts to cover is some of the most important, and the most difficult to teach, of any in the book. If our students acquire nothing else from their study of quantitative methods, they should at least gain some kind of intelligent 'feel' for numerical data.

There is no substitute here for practical experience – newspaper articles and items in radio and television news broadcasts regularly provide material for discussion. Two exercises which I have found useful are.

1 Get students to estimate, in rough terms, a quantity such as the likely weekly takings of a local supermarket; the height of a nearby multi-storey building; or the number of entries in a telephone directory. If they write down their estimates independently, huge variations generally appear. These can be resolved by discussing suitable approximate methods for arriving at the answers. For example, how tall is the average person? How much taller than that is one floor of a building? Therefore, roughly how high will a building of six floors be? Do we need to add anything extra? And so on. This exercise helps develop a feel for what are, and are not, 'sensible' figures in a given situation.

2 The Mathematical Association's publication, *Mathematical Gazette*, includes at the foot of many of its pages misleading or peculiar numerical statements gleaned from the media. The Royal Statistical Society's *RSS News* also contains a selection of this kind, under the title 'Forsooth'. Getting students to think about these items, and to identify precisely why they are silly, misleading, etc. can be an interesting exercise.

Chapter 5
TABLES AND DIAGRAMS

Outline content

This chapter covers:
- **tabulation and diagrams for qualitative data (bar charts, pie charts, pictograms);**
- **tabulations and diagrams for quantitative data (ungrouped, grouped and cumulative frequency tables, histograms and ogives);**
- **simple numerical graphs, including scattergraphs and stepped graphs.**

Teaching this material

Many students will have covered the material of this chapter before, at some level, and this can be a mixed blessing. In particular, most will not clearly appreciate the distinction between histograms and bar charts, and will believe that the vertical scale of a histogram represents frequency (never before having encountered histograms for unequally-grouped data). If this idea is not sorted out at this stage, it can lead to problems later when the vertical scale of a normal curve may be interpreted as giving a probability.

Another common area of confusion is the plotting of ogives with points at the class mid-interval rather than the upper class limit (for a 'less than' ogive). This can be circumvented by encouraging students always to write out a cumulative frequency table *separately* from the original frequency table, rather than appending cumulative frequencies as an additional column in the latter.

Many of the ideas introduced here, like those of Chapter 2, may be dismissed as 'obvious' or even insultingly elementary, especially by mature students accustomed to producing reports containing bar charts, pie charts, etc. It is worthwhile having a collection of horrible bits of data presentation culled from the media (unfortunately such a collection does not take long to accumulate!) in order to demonstrate how information can be conveyed in more or less effective ways. The book *Plain Figures* by Chapman (HMSO) contains much thought-provoking material which illustrates that, even when there is no one 'right' way to construct a table or diagram, there is often a 'best' way for the particular purpose in hand.

Exploration of these ideas is, of course, now made much easier by the availability of software packages with high-quality graphics capability. Students should be encouraged to try several different versions of a table or chart on-screen, and discuss the pros and cons of each layout. They also need to develop a critical eye when using such software; as mentioned in the book, the use of a three-dimensional format for a bar chart does not always enhance clarity; bar charts may also masquerade as histograms, and so on.

Again, the exchanging of different versions of diagrams by groups of students for constructive comment can be helpful. Just as with questionnaires, no diagram or table is ever going to be beyond criticism. The important point is that there is no 'right answer', but that different formats bring out different features of the data.

One aspect of data tabulation which looms large in some professional exam syllabi, but which I have touched on fairly lightly, is the subject of 'true class boundaries', and the 'optimum' number of classes for a grouped frequency distribution given by Sturges' rule (*see*, for example, Daniel and Terrell, (1986) *Business Statistics*, Houghton Mifflin, (4th edn) p.13). I would take the view that it is more important for students to get used to thinking about each data set on its own merits, and to making choices accordingly, than to learn to apply ill-understood 'rules'.

Solutions to the exercises

1   The table below could be elaborated by inclusion of various percentages (e.g. percentage regular/occasional/dormant for home/overseas). However, if these figures are included they need to be clearly distinguished from the actual data.

Breakdown of customers

	Home	*Overseas*	*Total*	
Regular	6,720	1,650	7,920	
Occasional	2,860	1,100	3,960	
Dormant	770	550	1,320	
Total	9,900	3,300	13,200	(last year's total: 11,000)

(*Source*: Company report)

2   Two possible versions of this diagram are shown (Figs 5.1 and 5.2). The bar chart is probably preferable since it could be argued that to show the difference in the total number of home and overseas customers, 'pies' of differing sizes should be used, though most graphics software does not easily accommodate this.

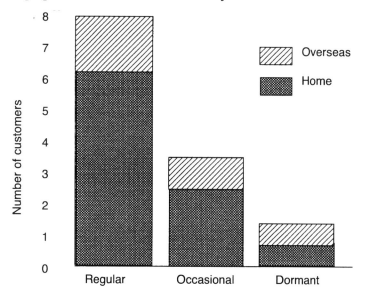

Fig. 5.1 Customer breakdown

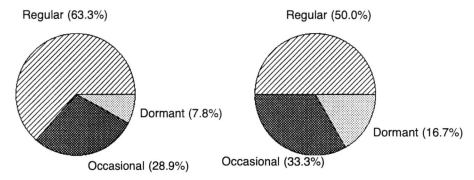

Fig. 5.2 Customer breakdown – home and overseas

3 A possible diagram is shown in Fig. 5.3, and an alternative version produced using Excel is given in Fig. 5.4. Strictly speaking, we should also show the 895 bills from the sample which contained no errors. The difficulty with this, as Fig. 5.5 indicates, is that a scale sufficiently large to accommodate this group makes the other groups appear almost meaninglessly small.

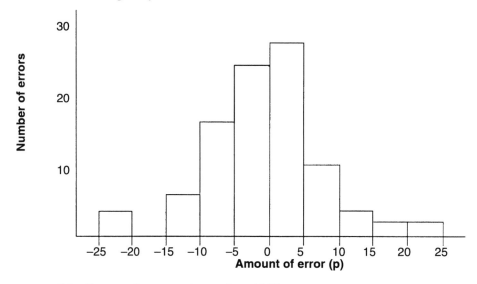

Fig. 5.3 Possible diagram for errors in receipted bills

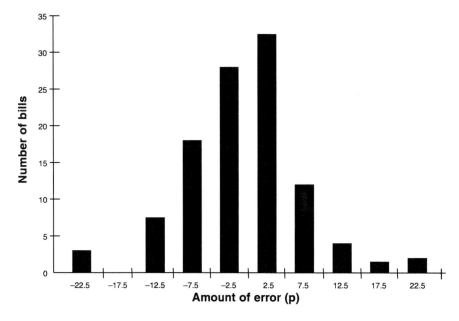

Fig. 5.4 Excel version of diagram for errors in receipted bills

12

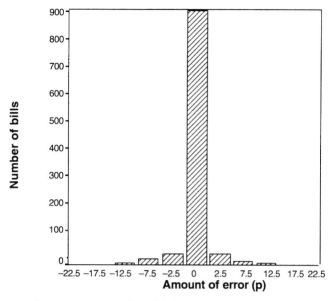

Fig. 5.5   Diagram for errors in receipted bills including zero

4   The most obvious tabulation is grouped in 10-mile ranges:

Miles travelled	No. of respondents
Less than 10	5
10 but under 20	11
20 but under 30	14
30 but under 40	7
40 but under 50	2
50 but under 60	1

If the information that there were no respondents from within a 5-mile radius is considered of particular interest, the version given in the solution at the back of the book may be preferable. It may also be worth looking at the 5-mile range version, which gives a much more 'spotty' impression.

5   The graph should of course be a step-function.

8   (a)   The frequency distribution is as shown; this example was produced using Excel.

AGE	FEMALES	MALES
under 25	1	0
25 but < 27	1	2
27 but < 29	8	15
29 but < 31	3	22
31 but < 33	7	18
33 but < 35	7	14
35 but < 37	8	7
37 but < 39	7	4
39 but < 41	5	3
41 but < 43	7	3
43 and over	1	0
Total	55	88

Since the sizes of the two groups are quite different, it might be desirable to include additional columns giving the percentage of the group in each age-band, for comparative purposes.

One possible diagram is given in Fig. 5.6. This is not ideal since (a) there should, of course, be no gaps between the bars – this is a histogram, not a bar-chart; and (b) the male–female comparison is not easy – what the diagram emphasises is rather the split of each age-band between male and female. A multiple (side-by-side) bar chart might be preferable if it is the gender comparison we wish to stress. This can be made into a point for discussion.

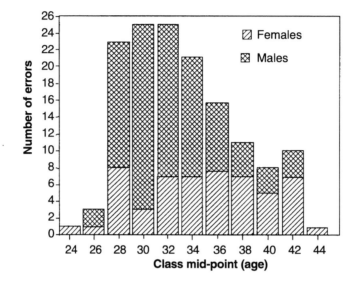

Fig. 5.6   Male/female age breakdown for STUD data

(c) The cross-tabulation of gender against first-degree subject produced by Excel is as follows:

SUBJECT	FEMALE	%	MALE	%
BUS/ECON	33	60.0	27	30.7
ENG	3	5.5	42	47.7
SCI	11	20.0	13	14.8
ARTS	8	14.5	6	6.8
	55	100.0	88	100.0

Columns showing the percentage of each gender group in the subject area have been added, since an obvious point of interest here is the difference between the proportions of men and women studying engineering, arts, and so on.

The identical information as produced by MINITAB looks rather different:

```
MTB > table c3 c4;
SUBC> count;
SUBC> rowp.
```

ROWS: GENDER   COLUMNS: SUBJECT

	1	2	3	4	All
0	33	3	11	8	55
	60.00	5.45	20.00	14.55	100.00
1	27	42	13	6	88
	30.68	47.73	14.77	6.82	100.00
ALL	60	45	24	14	143
	41.96	31.47	16.27	9.79	100.00

CELL CONTENTS -

COUNT
% OF ROW

If we wish to emphasise the breakdown by subject, and ignore the difference in overall size of the two groups, pie charts are a possibility for presenting this data, as shown in Fig.5.7. However, various forms of bar chart could also be used.

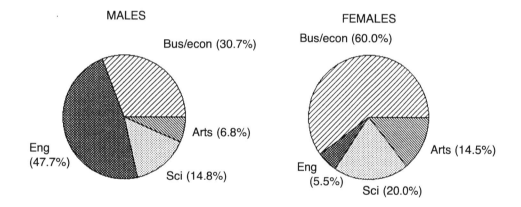

Fig. 5.7 Subject by gender

Given that the diagrams are to be used in a presentation to potential students, some discussion can be generated on the impression given by the various layouts, and which format might be preferred by (i) the course management, and (ii) the audience.

9 The data produces the cumulative frequency table shown; the <= format is dictated by the way the Excel function works. The l-gm class interval perhaps leads to rather a large number of classes; however, a 2-gm interval is somewhat coarse for machines 1 and 3 with their small dispersions.

It may be useful to link the appearance of the ogives with the behaviour of the data – a steep increase at the start corresponding to a large number of values at the lower end of the weight spectrum, and so on.

WEIGHT	MACH 1	MACH 2	MACH 3
< = 244	0	0	0
< = 245	0	1	0
< = 246	0	3	6
< = 247	0	15	22
< = 248	4	25	56
< = 249	15	39	88
< = 250	52	56	98
< = 251	82	67	100
< = 252	98	77	
< = 253	99	87	
< = 254	100	94	
< = 255		96	
< = 256		98	
< = 257		100	

The corresponding ogives appear as in Fig. 5.8.

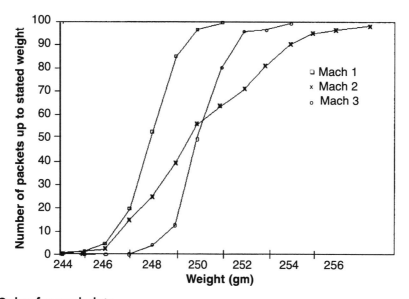

Fig. 5.8 Ogive for mach data

10 The scattergraphs shown in Figs 5.9(a) and (b) have floorspace as the horizontal and takings as the vertical axis, but for the purposes of the scattergraph this is not important. Fig. 5.9(a) was produced by MINITAB, and Fig. 5.9(b) by Excel. The general impression is that, while there is a tendency as one might expect for larger stores to generate larger takings, there are also many other factors producing considerable scatter in the data.

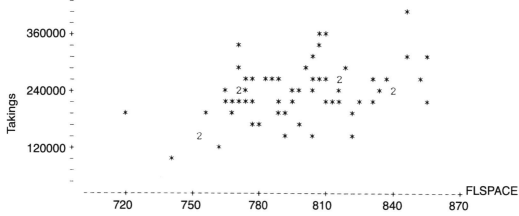

Fig. 5.9 (a) Scattergraph from QUAL data

16

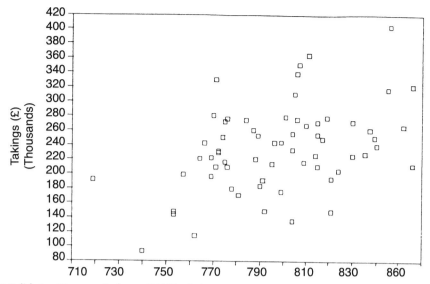

Fig. 5.9 (b) Scattergraph from QUAL data

11 This data can be presented in a wide range of ways; one possibility (the version given in the Solutions at the back of the book) is shown below:

Company name	No. of shares at start	No. of shares at end	Change during year	Income/ expenditure (£)
Equimix plc	500	0	−500	650
Farringdon Holdings	800	1000	+200	(160)
Greenbridge	400	200	−200	160
Heavicast Ltd	0	400	+400	(288)

Surplus for the year = £326

It is difficult, and probably not very useful, to devise a diagram which attempts to show all the information at once; it is perhaps preferable to use separate diagrams for subsets of the data. Thus the bar charts below contrast the holdings at the start and end of the year:

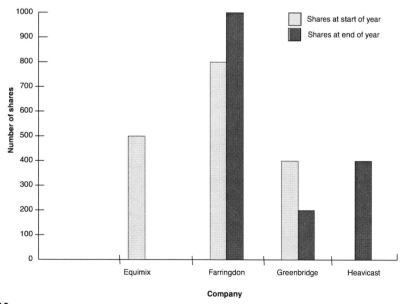

Fig. 5.10

17

The pie charts in Fig. 5.11 can be shown to show the percentage makeup of the portfolio at the start and the end of the year.

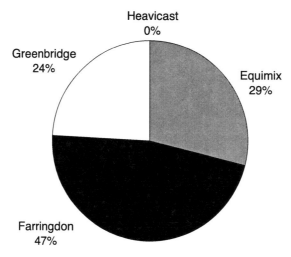

Fig. 5.11 (a) Portfolio at start of year

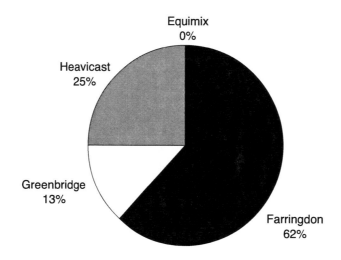

Fig. 5.11 (b) Portfolio at end of year

12 The suggested solution given in the book is as follows, though as usual there are numerous other possibilities:

| | No. of responses (% of row) | | | |
	Good	Fair	Poor	Total
Car owners	230 (66)	72 (21)	45 (13)	347 100)
Non-car owners	29 (20)	51 (36)	63 (44)	143 (100)
Total	259 (53)	123 (25)	108 (22)	490 (1100

The percentages have been given row-wise to emphasise the difference in the way opinions split between the two groups of customers. Given the difference in the size of the two groups, one could either use a straight bar chart to show the results, as in Fig. 5.12(a) or a percentage bar chart, as in Fig. 5.12(b).

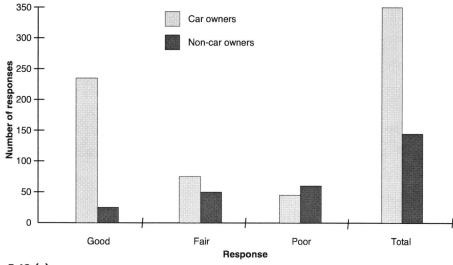

Fig. 5.12 (a)

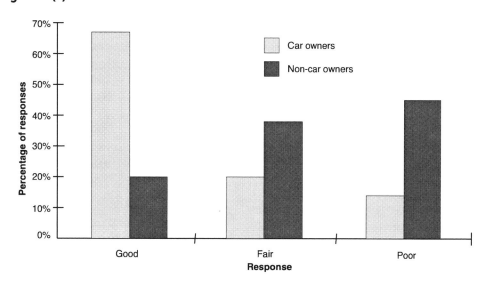

Fig. 5.12 (b)

The different impressions given in the two charts can lead to some interesting discussion.

Suggestions for further work

Questions 6 and 7 of the exercises contain a couple of ideas on further work. With the advent of more and more sophisticated graphics packages, the use of graphic data presentation in the media is exploding – and the number of instances of poor presentation seems to be increasing at a more than proportionate rate. Other sources of material apart from those already mentioned include company reports; the Consumers' Association magazine *Which?*; and publications of Trade Unions and professional associations (especially those produced in connection with wage negotiations).

If software packages are being extensively used to produce graphics, it is important that the particular package available does not become a straitjacket, determining the presentation method chosen to the possible detriment of effective communication. I would always want to include an element of hand-sketching of diagrams, if only to provide a model towards which one can work with the aid of the package.

Chapter 6
MEASURES OF LOCATION AND SPREAD

Outline content

This chapter covers calculation and interpretation of the standard summary statistics for a set of measured data - mean, standard deviation, variance, median and quartiles, mode and range.

Teaching this material

There are still two schools of thought as to the teaching of summary statistics. Some adhere to the view that students should be able to hand-calculate the measures even if they will generally be making use of a statistical package to perform computations. Others feel that all that is now required is for students to be able to make sensible use of a measure obtained from a computer printout. I have attempted to steer a middle course, eschewing a totally 'black box' attitude to what goes on inside the statistical package while seeing little point in laborious hand-calculation with anything more than the simplest of datasets – just sufficient to acquire some 'feel' for what is going on.

The standard deviation needs a special mention here. It is doubtful if any student who has encountered this measure for the first time really has a clear idea of what the s.d. is, however good the teaching she has received. Engineering students are sometimes at a slight advantage here, since the concept of a root–mean–square may be familiar to them from electrical theory. I think the best which can be done at the initial stage is to try to develop an idea of s.d. in a comparative context, and to use interpretations such as '95 per cent of values in a fairly symmetrically distributed population can be expected to be within about two s.ds either side of the mean' to build up a picture of how the s.d. may be useful. Further understanding comes with use of the Normal distribution tables.

There is also the question of division by n versus n-1 in computing the s.d. Many calculators now offer both forms of calculation, so the question cannot be ducked. I have attempted in the chapter to give a brief explanation of the distinction; the main need for beginning students is to be consistent, and to ensure that formulae used for hand-computation agree with the results of any statistical packages being used, so that students do not become confused.

Note on the worksheet MSD.XLS

This Excel worksheet, as indicated in the text, contains the necessary formulae for calculating the mean and standard deviation 'from first principles' – that is, without recourse to Excel statistical functions. The example data used is the wage data for Grimchester workers taken from p. 89 of the text. Students should be encouraged to explore this worksheet, and relate the formulae in the cells to the process of computing a mean and standard deviation by hand.

It is also interesting to experiment with the effect of outliers on the values of the mean and standard deviation, by altering the mid-point of the top or bottom class.

The data can be overwritten, so that the worksheet may be used with other datasets; however, if the frequency table contains more than nine rows, additional rows will need to be added to the main table, and the formulae modified accordingly.

Solutions to the exercises

1 The solutions given at the back of the book assume that the upper limit of the distribution is £200,000. Further details of calculations are:

Barsetshire

Class	x	f	fx	fx^2	cum f
> 65 but < 70	67.5	2	55	1512.5	2
> 70 but < 75	72.5	5	162.5	5281.25	7
> 75 but < 80	77.5	12	450	16875	19
> 80 but < 90	85	20	900	40500	39
> 90 but < 100	100	14	840	50400	53
> 110 but < 140	115	6	510	43350	59
140 and more	150	1	150	22500	60
Sum		60	3067.5	180418.7	

Mean	=	51.125
s.d.	=	19.82961
Median	=	45.5
Ql	=	38.33333
Q2	=	58.57142

Cokeshire

Class	x	f	fx	fx^2	cum f
> 25 but < 30	27.5	4	110	3025	4
> 30 but < 35	32.5	11	357.5	11618.75	15
> 35 but < 40	37.5	19	712.5	26718.75	34
> 40 but < 50	45	15	675	30375	49
> 50 but < 70	60	6	360	21600	55
> 70 but < 100	85	4	340	28900	59
100 and more	150	1	150	22500	60
Sum		60	2705	144737.5	

Mean	=	45.08333
s.d.	=	19.48806
Median	=	38.94736
Q1	=	35
Q2	=	47.33333

If the s.d. with n-1 divisor is used, the values are £19,997 for Barsetshire and £19,683 for Cokeshire.

Both distributions are somewhat skew, with long tails at the upper end (positive skew). This is reflected in the fact that means are greater than medians, and Ql is closer to the median than Q3. The 'typical' house price for Barsetshire is greater than that for Cokeshire, whichever measure is used – in fact, roughly speaking, 50 per cent of houses in Cokeshire cost less than £39,000, whereas only 25 per cent of houses in Barsetshire cost less than £38,000. The variability of prices is also greater in Barsetshire (measured by s.d. or interquartile range).

Possible discussion points include the appropriateness of using the same closing value for the top class in both distributions, and the effect this may have on the measures and the conclusions we can draw from them.

2 For the first set of data, $\Sigma x = 32$ $\Sigma x^2 = 242$

Mean = 6.4   Standard deviation = $\sqrt{(242/5 - 6.4^2)}$
                                  = 2.72
            (if n-1 divisor is used, s.d. = 3.05)

For the second set of data, $\Sigma x = 132$ $\Sigma x^2 = 3522$

Mean = 26.4   Standard deviation = $\sqrt{(3522/5 - 26.4^2)}$
                                  = 2.72
            (if n-1 divisor is used, s.d. = 3.05)

So adding 20 to each data value adds 20 to the mean, but leaves the s.d. unchanged. This can be illustrated by reference to Fig. 6.1 below. More capable students can generalise this result into the form:

$$\text{mean } (x + a) = a + \text{mean } (x)$$
$$\text{s.d. } (x + a) = \text{s.d. } (x)$$

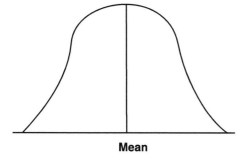 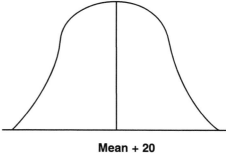

Mean   **Mean + 20**

Fig. 6.1   Distribution diagrams relating to practical exercise 2

3 The first set of data is identical with that in question 2 above.

For the second set, $\Sigma x = 96$ $\Sigma x^2 = 2178$

Mean = 19.2   Standard deviation = $\sqrt{(2178/5 - 19.2^2)}$
                                  = 8.18
            (with n-1 divisor s.d. = 9.15)

Thus multiplying all the data values by 3 multiplies both the mean and s.d. by 3. Again, this can be generalised:

$$\text{mean } (kx) = k \text{ mean } (x)$$
$$\text{s.d. } (kx) = k \text{ s.d. } (x)$$

The principles established in these two questions form the basis of the 'coded variable' method for hand-calculation of mean and s.d., still described in many texts. While it is now hardly worthwhile burdening students with the additional formulae such texts use with coding, it is still helpful, even if a calculator is being used, to be aware that for example one can informally 'knock off 1000' from very large data values, to save on handling of large figures, and then 'add it back' to the mean at the end of the process.

4   A nice example of the kind of thing needed for this exercise is provided by the *Sunday Times* (23 April 1989, quoted in Royal Statistical Society's *News and Notes*, Sept 89) writing about the University Teachers' pay dispute: '... the great bulk are stuck well below the median'. Since wage distributions are typically positively skewed, presumably this should have been '...below the mean'.

5   The usual example cited for use of the mode is sizing of garments, but there are others. In ergonomic design of equipment, for example, a car designer should be interested in modal leg length when designing the seat/pedal arrangement (hopefully in conjunction with the range).

6   Summary measures for the three machines are as shown, though it would not be necessary to incorporate all of these into the report.

MEAN	249.95	249.92	247.83
STAN	1.08	2.55	1.05
MAX	253.21	256.63	250.04
MIN	247.28	244.82	245.34
RANGE	5.93	11.81	4.70
MEDIAN	249.95	249.74	247.83
Q1	249.28	248.02	247.18
Q3	250.65	251.91	248.57

The most notable features are as follows:

(a)   Machine 3 is producing a weight on average about two grams lower than either of the other machines. This raises questions about the target weight to which the machines have been set. The medians give the same picture.

(b)   Machine 2 is much more inconsistent than the other two machines in the weights that it produces, with a s.d. and range which are more than twice as great. This clearly has implications for the company: if too many 'overweight' packets are being produced, product is effectively being 'given away', while too many underweight is a problem for legal reasons. Perhaps machine 2 is an older machine which cannot be so accurately set as the other two.

(c)   Machine 2's output is also quite skewed, with a longer tail on the right-hand side (positive skew).

The results of this exercise can be related to the cumulative frequency tables and ogives produced in Exercise 9 of Chapter 5. They can also be used as the basis of a preliminary discussion of the contribution statistics has to make to quality control: What is the consequence if a process has a large variability as measured by the s.d.? Once we've got a process set on target, how can we make sure it is not drifting away? Would it be possible to change the mean of a process without changing the s.d. also? And so on.

The features which I would hope to see in a report on this data would be commonsense interpretation of the figures (as in 'the variability of machine 2 is about twice that of the other two' rather than quoting s.d.'s to 4 decimal places); integration of the numbers into the overall report; and reference to the actual situation – the fact that these are machines filling packets – rather than treating the data as abstract figures.

7 The situation involved in answering this question is typical of that in which many users of statistical software find themselves. The MINITAB results deliberately include terms (TRMEAN and SEMEAN) which will be unfamiliar to students at this stage – they need to pick out the relevant measures from the irrelevant. (TRMEAN is actually the trimmed mean, with the largest and smallest 5 per cent of data omitted, while SEMEAN is, of course, the standard error of the mean.)

The major point to look for in a report based on this data is a sensible explanation of the measures in simple language. There is no need for every single figure to be used simply because it is there. With this data, the notable features are that hospital 2 exhibits both a longer average wait and greater variability than hospital 1, and that in the case of hospital 1 there is along upper tail to the distributioan (median-Q1 less than Q3-median), while for hospital 2 the reverse seems to be true – even though the longest wait in hospital 2 is much longer than in hospital 1.

There is probably no need to mention the wrods 'standard deviation' in the report at all; much better to say things such as 'half the patients at hospital 1 had to wait more than 10 weeks for their operation'.

Overall, the hallmarks of a good report should be

● brevity
● figures are used to support a conclusion, not merely stated without comment
● avoidance of technical statistical terms is avoided.

Suggestions for further work

At this stage it is useful to pick up any results generated by the survey work of Chapter 3, and do some data presentation/report writing in that context. Oral presentation of results is also useful since the techniques which make for a clear written report do not necessarily lead to a good oral presentation, and vice versa. The *suitability* of the level and style of presentation to the audience also needs to be emphasised.

Chapter 7
INDEX NUMBERS

Outline content

This chapter covers:
- **the construction of base-weighted and current-weighted indices, concentrating on price indices;**
- **the application and interpretation of index numbers;**
- **an introduction to the General Index of Retail Prices.**

Teaching this material

In many ways the material of this chapter might sit more easily in an Economics course, especially those sections concerned with the pros and cons of different methods of index number construction. It is unlikely that students will ever be in the position of constructing an index from scratch – at least a complex weighted average type of index. However, this is still required material in many statistics courses – particularly for professional bodies' examinations. For the rest, however, an understanding of, rather than a proficiency in, the details of Laspeyres and Paasche calculations is probably adequate.

The use and interpretation of indices is a different matter. The Retail Price Index, the *Financial Times Ordinary Share Index* (FTOSI) and others are frequently in the news, and students need a good grasp of how indices can be used to deflate monetary values, and what an 'index-linked pension' implies.

The content of this chapter is not technically difficult – nor is it particularly fascinating lecture material – and I have found the exercise outlined in question 5 in the practical exercises invaluable in motivating students towards this topic (see solution 5 below). Incidentally, this exercise also forms a good basis for the development of spreadsheet skills.

Note on the worksheet INDEX.XLS

This Excel worksheet contains the necessary formulae for computing base- and current-weighted price indices, using the data on page 130 as an illustration. Students may find it helpful to explore the worksheet, relating the cell contents to the various elements of the formulae. It is also interesting to see how many decimal places one needs to include in the final indices before any difference between base and current-weighting shows up.

The worksheet can also be overwritten with data relating to other exercises, though if more than three items are to be included, additional rows will need to be added to the basic calculation. It can also be modified to yield volume or value indices as well as price indices, simply by adding the relevant formulae – all the components are already present.

Solutions to the exercises

1

	1991		1992		p_0q_0	p_0q_1	p_1q_0	p_1q_1
	Price p_0 (p)	Quantity q_0 (000)	Price p_1 (p)	Quantity q_0 (000)				
Beer (pt)	130	60	140	55	7800	7150	8400	7700
Whisky (sgl)	165	20	180	21	3300	3485	3600	3780
Tomato juice (sml)	55	15	75	18	825	990	1125	1350
					11925	11605	13125	12830

Base-weighted (Laspeyres) price   = 1.10063
Current-weighted (Paasche) price index = 1.10556

So, to nearest per cent, Laspeyres is 110, Paasche is 111

2

Year	Turnover (actual)	RPI	Turnover (deflated to '88 values)
1988	16	108.9	16.00
1989	18	115.2	16.70
1990	22	126.1	18.65

3 The rise in the RPI was actually only 20/245 = 8.2 per cent. An increase of 20 percentage points (i.e. 20 per cent of the base-year value) must not be confused with a 20 per cent increase. It is worth mentioning the Japanese share price (Nikkei) average in this context – this typically has values around the 4000 mark, so that changes from day to day can sound enormous, but expressed as percentage changes they are, in fact, trivial.

4 This question gives an opportunity to discuss whether the RPI is the right deflator to use in a given company context, and if not, what other index might be used instead.

5 This is the 'student cost of living index' exercise mentioned above. There is a tremendous amount of mileage to be got out of this exercise – if students have access to a spreadsheet, the data can be collected there and updated weekly to give current estimates of the weights and index. It can also be presented diagrammatically.

There will be plenty of problems for discussion. For example, some students pay rent which includes heat and light; some colleges collect rent termly, so it must be decided whether that amount should only be included in the week in which it is paid, or spread evenly over the weeks of term. How can we select 'representative' food prices? And so on. Brighter students will be able to cope with an algebraic demonstration that the weighted average of price relatives is equivalent to a base-weighted price index.

There are also non-statistical benefits to the exercise. Some students have never carried out a budgeting exercise of this kind, and are surprised – and sometimes alarmed – to discover where their money goes! For mature students the exercise will of course need modifying somewhat. They can discuss what to do about their mortgage repayments, which can lead to a discussion of RPI versus the Tax and Prices Index (TPI).

Overseas students can also contribute to the discussion information about how inflation is measured in their home countries.

6 The solutions to parts (a)–(c) are given below, as indicated:

Year	A	(a) A index	(c) A chain	B	(b) B index	(c) B chain
1987	23	100		82	100	
1988	25	109	109	85	104	104
1989	28	122	112	91	111	107
1990	31	135	111	94	115	103
1991	35	152	113	99	121	105
1992	39	170	111	102	124	103
1993	44	191	113	108	132	106
1994	50	217	114	114	139	106

The solution to part (d) is as follows:

Year	RPI	A	A deflated	A def index	A def chain	B	B deflated	B def index	B def chain
1987	115.00	23	23.00	100		82	82	100	
1988	117.00	25	24.57	107	107	85	83.55	102	102
1989	118.20	28	27.24	118	111	91	88.54	108	106
1990	118.90	31	29.98	130	110	94	90.92	111	103
1991	119.50	35	33.68	146	112	99	95.27	116	105
1992	121.00	39	37.07	161	110	102	96.94	118	102
1993	122.30	44	41.37	180	112	108	101.55	124	105
1994	124.00	50	46.37	202	112	114	105.73	129	104

(e) Both the raw and deflated figures show that, though company A makes far smaller profits than B, its rate of growth is greater. The index series based on 1987 give growth compared with that year; the deflated series give a somewhat less optimistic pciture than those based on the raw figures.

The chain index series are suitable for estimating the year-on year growth rates of the companies, ranging from 9–14 per cent for A and from 3–7 per cent for B. Again deflation leads to somewhat reduced rates.

Discussion of these results could focus around the fact that all these different series, all honestly obtained from the data, offer scope for considerable variation in the view taken of results.

Suggestions for further work

Monitoring a rapidly-fluctuating index such as the FTOSI can provide an interesting exercise, particularly if the prices of the individual shares which go to make it up are also monitored – the effect of individual changes on the overall index can then be assessed.

There is also scope for joint work with Economics, and perhaps with Accounting in terms of Inflation Accounting

Chapter 8
ELEMENTARY PROBABILITY

Outline content

This chapter covers:
- **basic definitions of probability;**
- **probability computations using multiplication and addition rules;**
- **the concept of expected value;**
- **very simple decision theory using tables and trees.**

Teaching this material

Many students will find the material of this chapter some of the most demanding in the entire book. There is really no substitute for practice on examples when it comes to acquiring the 'mental set' required to tackle probability problems and, because the topic does not lend itself to the laying down of standard methods, this problem-solving can be a painful process.

We need to realise, however, that there is a difference between having a grasp of what a probability indicates and being proficient in dealing with complex problems – and that the latter is not really required by students whose main aim is to understand hypothesis testing and sampling. Certainly, I would not regard details of permutations and combinations in connection with probability calculations as appropriate for such students – and have therefore not included them in the book.

Many less able students can relate much more easily to 'numbers of occurrences' or even proportions than to probabilities expressed in four-figures decimals, and I generally choose to deal with Bayes' Theorem-type problems on this basis. In fact, the interchangeability of the ideas of probability/proportion/ percentage is one of the major points to get across at this stage.

Solutions to the exercises

1 This can be broken down piecemeal thus:

p(sink clear) $= 1 - p$(sink blocked) $= 1 - 1/3 = 2/3$
p(towel) $= 1 - 2/5 = 3/5$
p(sink clear and towel) $= 2/3 \times 3/5 = 2/5 = 0.4 = 40\%$

There are several points to be made here:

p(not A) $= 1 - p$(A),

saying 'on average one day out of three' is using the second (relative frequency or empirical) definition of probability, and so on.

2 Since the data is subdivided into two sets of categories, a table provides the simplest line of approach:

	Male	*Female*	*Total*
F/t	450	300	750
P/t	50	200	250
Total	500	500	1,000

Note that the total figure of 1,000 has been assumed here purely for the sake of convenience in calculation – overall it is *proportions*, not actual numbers, with which we are concerned.

Then (a) p(worker is male) = 500/1000 = 50 per cent; (b) p(part-time worker is male) = 20 per cent (these two could quite easily be done without the table); and (c) p(male worker is part-time) = 50/500 = 10 per cent.

(In (b) and (c) we have some further information about the worker – namely, that he is male/part-time – so the denominator of the probability is reduced. Another way of wording this would be 'given that the worker is male, what is the probability that he is part-time'. This is really a posterior probability by any other name.)

3 (a) p(both alive) = p(MM alive and AA alive) = (4/5) × (95/100) = 0.76

 (b) 'One or the other but not both' can be decomposed into 'AA alive and MM dead or AA dead and MM alive' = (95/100 × 1/5) + (5/100 × 4/5) = 23/100 = 0.23.

A point to make here is that we are decomposing the basic question into mutually exclusive cases.

4 (a) The quickest way of doing this is to work from the opposite case:

   p(detected) = 1 − p(undetected)
   But p(undetected) = p(all three miss the error)
   = 1/5 × 2/5 × 1/2 = 1/25 = 0.04. So p(detected) = 0.96.

   It can also be done in a more long-winded fashion:

   p(first detects or first fails and second detects or first two fail and third detects)
   = 4/5 + (1/5 × 3/5) + (1/5 × 2/5 × 1/2) = 24/25 = 0.96.

   A tree diagram could be used for this.

 (b) The success rates of the three cannot be compared because they are looking at different sets – the last sees a set of the most difficult cases, which the other two have failed to detect.

5 Two popular errors:
   p(one fails) = 4/12.

This does not work because we have not taken into account what happens to the other two – they might fail too, in which case we would not have just one failure as required.

p(one fails, the other two pass) = 4/12 × 8/11 × 7/10.

This assumes that it is the first one which fails. The correct answer is, of course:

(4/12 × 8/11 × 7/10) + (8/12 × 4/11 × 7/10) + (8/12 × 7/11 × 4/10),

which is equivalent to:

4/12 × 8/11 × 7/10 × 3 = 0.51.

6 This is best done via a pay-off table:

	Job moves	*Job stays*	*EMV*
Move house	250	200	220
Stay	200	300	260
Probability	0.4	0.6	

The minimum EMV solution is to move.

It could be debated whether EMV is an appropriate method to use for this one-off decision; also the EMVs are quite close, so the problem could be sensitive to small changes in the estimated costs and probabilities.

7 A very simple tree can be drawn:

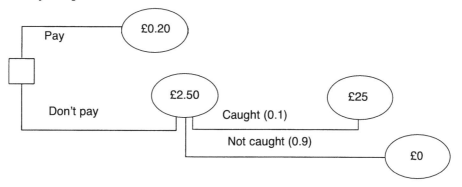

Fig. 8.1

Thus on the EMV criterion it is cheaper to pay! The 'long-run' EMV approach is quite suitable here.

8 The tree diagram below shows that selling now is the maximum EMV option – but again, the use of this criterion could be debated.

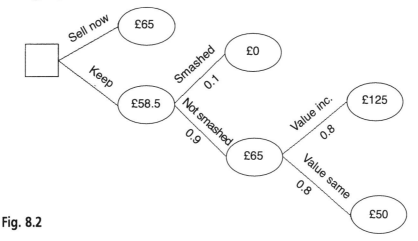

Fig. 8.2

31

9 (a) This is the problem addressed by opinion polls; most students will know something about these – and their dubious accuracy. So this question can be used to lead into a preliminary discussion of how well sample data represents a population, preparatory to work in Chapter 10.

(b) This question could be done empirically by looking at published birth figures. But how constant is the male:female birth ratio over the country? Are there any other relevant factors we need to take into account?

(c) An actual experiment could be done here – but it would only be based on a sample, so how reliable will the figure obtained be?

(d) You can look up data on plane accidents per 1,000 miles flown – but different airlines have different safety records. In any case, the probabilities are very low; so why do people worry so much about air crashes? This can open up a discussion of other 'low probability, serious consequence' events, such as failures in nuclear reactors. How can we attach a probability to an event which has never yet been seen to happen?

10 Plotting a graph of the cumulative probability, preferably via a computer package, makes this a more entertaining exercise.

11 If we call the probability that the series appears p, then the EMV of the decision to go ahead is:

$$p \times 15 - (1-p) \times 1 = 16p - 1$$

So even when p takes its smallest value of 0, this EMV is only -1, as compared with -5 for abandoning the project now. Thus, it is always worth going ahead.

12 If the probability of discovery is p, then the EMV of not paying is £25p. For this to be preferable to paying, we need $25p < 0.2$, i.e. $p < 0.008$ or 2/250.

Conversely, if the probabilities are as in the question, but the meter charge is £x, then for not paying to be preferable we need £2.50 $< x$, so unless the charge goes up to £2.50 it will be worth trying to get away without paying.

(Some students who don't like the abstraction of ps and xs may prefer to see their way through these problems by less formal means – or, for sensitivity in more complex examples, by 'trying' other values of p.)

13 The parts of the tree relating to the decisions 'go ahead' and 'abandon now' remain as before, with EMVs of £8,000 and $-$£5,000 respectively. The new branch for the decision 'do survey' is as shown below:

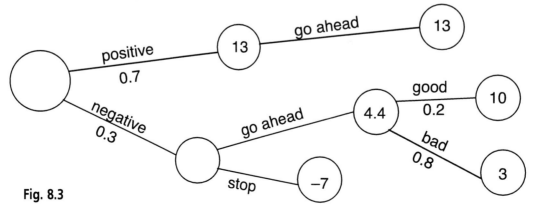

Fig. 8.3

Notice that as the figures given in the question are *profits*, we assume that the development and survey costs have already been deducted – though there is scope for argument here, and some students may interpret the question differently. Since profits are made even in the case of a bad survey, whereas there will be a £7,000 loss if the project is abandoned after the survey, the correct decision should the survey predict poor results is to go ahead anyway. The 'survey' branch of the tree can thus be modified as shown.

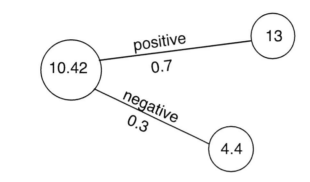

Fig. 8.4

This yields expected profits of £10,420 as against £8,600 from going ahead without a survey. The overall decision should therefore be 'do survey, but if it's negative, go ahead anyway'.

14 (a) It is simplest to see what is going on here if we assume that 1,000,000 people are tested for the disease, and set up a table to show the results:

	Has disease	Does not have disease	Total
Positive test	4.75	19,999.9	20,004.65
Negative test	0.25	979,995.1	979,995.35
Total	5	999,995	1,000,000

Thus p(have disease given positive test) = 4.75/20,004.65 = 0.00024 to 5 decimal places.

(b) This means that the porbability of actually having the disease, even if you test positive, is very small indeed, so that many people are going to be unnecessarily alarmed by their test result. This fact results from the combination of a failry inaccurate test and a very rare complaint. There are of course implications here about universal testing for illnesses such as AIDS, though the accuracy of real-life tests is usually better than in this example.

(c) The main assumption involved here is that the underlying rate of the disease in the population is known. There are likely to be reliable approximations to this figure available in the case of well-established and thoroughly investigated diseases, but probably not for complaints which have only recently been identified or which, like AIDS, are increasing in prevalence.

Suggestions for further work

Many students, particularly those with experience, will be highly critical of the EMV approach to decision making, as outlined here, regarding it as 'simplistic' (which of course it is). Some interesting discussion can ensue as to what alternative approach one might pursue – is 'intuition' or 'business experience' actually going to be any better as a guide? How could reliable probability estimates for future events be approximated in practice? Could you, for example, get a consensus estimate by asking an experienced group?

The assigning of monetary values also leads to interesting questions: how do you put a value on such imponderables as 'quality of environment' (the kind of question which needs to be addressed when, for example, deciding the line of a new motorway)? How can we quantify the fact that some people are 'risk-seekers' and others 'risk avoiders'?

A good reference for further work in this area – readable but not elementary in concepts – is *Decision Making* by Lindley.

There are numerous areas which have been in the news in recent years, and which provide good opportunities for a discussion of risk – the BSE scare, legal cases involving DNA evidence, and of course the National Lottery. Cases involving DNA evidence often hinge on an understanding of the difference between 'What is the probability that this person is guilty *given the evidence*?' and 'What is the probability of the evidence *given that this person is guilty*?', a subtlety which is worth some attention.

Chapter 9
SOME PROBABILITY DISTRIBUTIONS

Outline content

This chapter covers:
- **the characteristics of the three major probability distributions (Binomial, Poisson, Normal);**
- **the use of tables of the distributions to solve problems;**
- **the interconnections between the three distributions.**

Teaching this material

I believe there are two major sources of difficulty for students encountering this material for the first time:

- The problem of recognising which distribution is a good model in a given situation. I attempt to address this problem by stressing the features of the type of situation modelled by each distribution, and in particular the information (parameters) needed for each.
- The problem of actually using the tables. I have chosen to use cumulative Binomial and Poisson tables, which means that, say, to find p(exactly two occurrences), one has to take p(two or more) – p(one or more). However, whatever format of tables is chosen, this kind of manipulation of the figures will be required to find p(no less than 3), p(at least 5), and so on. For students who find this difficult, I find the use of a line diagram, as illustrated on page 153 of *Quantitative Approaches in Business Studies*, very helpful.

A similar difficulty can arise with Normal problems, and here students need to be encouraged always to sketch a diagram of the distribution, with the known data (mean, etc.) and the required area clearly marked.

As suggested in Chapter 8, it is often helpful to translate the four-figure decimals which emerge from the tables into more meaningful percentages. To say 'about two and a quarter per cent of the tubes are more than 200mm long' is a lot more meaningful than 'the probability of obtaining a tube more than 200mm long is 0.02275'.

I made a policy decision not to include formulae for Binomial and Poisson probabilities. It is possible to illustrate the Binomial concept with a simple example, as I do in the chapter, without involving combination formulae etc. As for Poisson, students at this level clearly cannot cope with Poisson as the result of a limiting process on a Binomial, and are also quite likely to be unfamiliar with the exponential function, so I do not believe that they will really benefit from knowing what the formula looks like.

Solutions to the exercises

1 Here since we do not know how many tomatoes are in a tray (they are probably packed by weight so the number will be variable), but may assume that the number is large, and the probability of a bad one small, we choose a Poisson model.

The mean can be calculated as 12/6 = 2 bad fruit per tray.

(a) p(2 or more bad) comes directly from Poisson tables with a mean of 2. The answer is 0.5940, or nearly 60 per cent; or, approximately, a 3 in 5 chance; or 'six in every ten trays will have two or more bad tomatoes'; and so on.

(b) p(no bad fruit) = p(exactly 0 bad) =
p(0 or more) $-p$(1 or more) = $1 - 0.8647 = 0.1353$.

2 The 'three in every twenty' sometimes deceives students into thinking that a group size of 20 is involved – but of course it's just another way of saying that:

p(no hat) = 3/20 = 0.15.

The relevant value of n here is 10.

p(exactly 3 with no hat) = p(3 or more) $- p$(4 or more) = $0.1797 - 0.0499 = 0.1298$
i.e., about a 13 per cent probability.

3 No problem in spotting this as Normal.

(a) $z = (4.7 - 5)/0.2 = -1.5$.
p(length $\leq$ 4.7) = $p(z \leq -1.5) = 0.0668$, or just over 6 1/2 per cent.

(b) $z = (4.8 - 5)/0.2 = -1$.
p(length $\geq$ 4.8) = $p(z \geq -1) = 1 - p(z \leq -1) =$
$1 - 0.1587 = 0.8413$.

(c) p(length between 4.6 and 5.3) =
$1 - p$(length below 4.6 or over 5.3) =
$1 - (p(z \leq -2) + p(z \geq 1.5)\} =$
$1 - (0.02275 + 0.0668) = 0.91045$.

(Students sometimes get hung up on the formalism of how they should write these computations, especially if they have done the subject before as part of a maths course. It is obviously important that what is written down should be clear and make sense, so statements such as

$x = 4.6 = z = -2 = 0.02275$

are to be discouraged. But personally, I do not worry too much about set ways of writing the computation out, so long as understanding is evident.)

4 The occurrence of the word 'average' in this question deceives some students into thinking it involves a Poisson distribution.

In fact it is Binomial, with p(late) = 0.25, $n = 5$

p(late less than 3 times) =
$1 - p$(late 3 or more times) =
$1 - 0.1035 = 0.0965$.

'Most likely' means the case with the highest probability.

p(late 0 times) = $1 - 0.7627 = 0.2373$
p(late once) = $0.7627 - 0.3672 = 0.3955$
p(late twice) = $0.3672 - 0.1035 = 0.2637$

So once is most likely – since the distribution is unimodal, there's no need to go any further.

(The expected number of times late is $0.25 \times 5 = 1.25$, so one might be tempted to round this off to 1 as the nearest feasible value. But does this always work? Try $n = 7$, $p = 0.25$.)

It might be interesting here to discuss whether the Binomial assumptions hold – would you expect probability of lateness to vary with the day of the week?

5 The z-value corresponding to a tail area of 0.15 in the Normal distribution is about 1.04. So we can say:

$1.04 = (13 - 10)/s$, whence $s = 2.88$ or roughly 3 min.

Some students, rather than manipulate the algebraic expression, may find it easier to say:

3 minutes (from 10 to 13) is 1.04 s.d.s, so one s.d. is just a bit less than 3 minutes.

6 Binomial again:

p(order) = 0.9, $n = 5$.

BUT $p = 0.9$ is not in the tables, so we need to invert the problem and express it in terms of failing to get an order p(fail) = 0.1.

Then:

p(4 orders from 5 quotes) = p(1 failure) =
p(1 or more) – p(2 or more) = $0.4094 - 0.0814 = 0.328$.

Students sometimes have an urge to subtract this from 1, on the grounds that they did so with the probability at the beginning. It needs to be emphasised that '4 orders' is the same situation as '1 fail'.

7 Poisson; if we are talking about a two-minute interval then we need the mean per two minutes, which is $12/5 \times 2 = 4.8$.

p(too many calls in two-minute interval) =
p(13 or more) = 0.0014 – which is a very small chance.

8 (a) proportion of rejects = $1,500/50,000 = 0.03$.
So p(value above 1,000 gm) = 0.03, which gives $z = 1.88$.
Thus $1.88 = (1,005 - 1,000)/s$, whence $s = 2.66$ gm.

Alternatively, as in question 5, say:

5 gm = 1.88 s.d.s – so how many gm is one s.d.?

(b) To save £40 at 8p per bag, we need to save $40/0.08 = 500$ rejected bags. Thus, the number of rejects must decrease to 1,000, and the proportion to $1,000/50,000 = 0.02$. Then $z = 2.05$, so mean – $1,000 = 2.05 \times 2.66$, whence mean = 1,005.45 gm.

(If the algebra goes wrong here, common sense should say that to reduce the proportion of underweight rejects, we need to increase the mean.)

9 (a) $n = 10$, $p = 0.5$ (assuming a fair coin)

$p(6$ or more$) = 0.3770$.

(b) $p($value greater than 5.5$) = p(z > 0.5/1.58) =$
$p(z > 0.32) = 0.3745$ – an error of less than 1 per cent.

(The idea of the continuity correction, though it is mentioned in the question, will probably need further discussion.)

10 (a) With $n = 10$, $p = 0.05$,

$p($at least 1 faulty$) = p(1$ or more faulty$) = 0.4013$.

(b) Using Poisson with mean $0.05 \times 10 = 0.5$,
$p(1$ or more$) = 0.3935$. Here the error is around 2 per cent.

11 Using a Normal approximation to the Poisson with mean 36 and s.d. = 6, and applying a continuity correction, we see that we need p(x<29.5). The corresponding value of z is (29.5–36)/6 = –1.083, and the probability is therefore 0.1394 (using MINITAB to obtain 3-figure accuracy on z).

There is thus about a 14 per cent chance that the 2,000m reel will have fewer than 30 flaws.

As always with Normal problems, it is helpful to students to sketch the relevant distribution here.

12 (a) This is a Binomial problem witn n = 10, and p = 0.05. We want p(0 defectives) which can be found from tables to be 1 – p(1 or more) = 0.5987 or nearly 60 per cent.

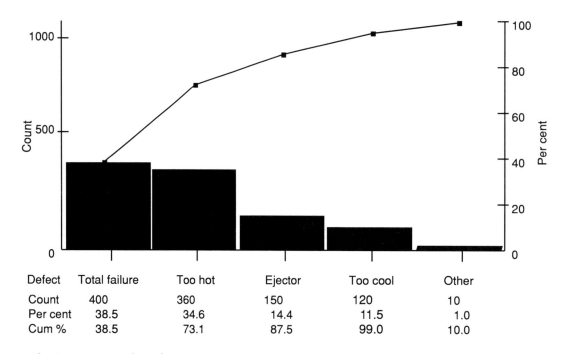

Defect	Total failure	Too hot	Ejector	Too cool	Other
Count	400	360	150	120	10
Per cent	38.5	34.6	14.4	11.5	1.0
Cum %	38.5	73.1	87.5	99.0	10.0

Fig. 9.1 Pareto chart for: C1

(b) and (c) are done in an exactly similar way with p = 0.1, 0.15, 0.2, giving probabilities of 0.3487, 0.1969 and 0.1074 respectively. The operating characteristic based on these figures is shown in Fig. 9.1:

This scheme is very crude, since when the rate of defective material is as high as 20 per cent over 10 per cent of batches are still being accepted. The main problem is the samll size of the sample – a larger sample would provide better information and allow more discrimination. If students have access to more extensive tables, or to software such as MINITAB which can generate probabilities for a binomial distribution, more realistic sample sizes can be investigated, and the impact of changing the sample size versus changing the acceptance number can be examined.

Students frequently espress the view that smpling inspection is a poor way of going about the inspection process, since it involves sending back good material as well as accepting some poor-quality items. Some, particularly those with some TQM expreience, may go so far as to claim that such methods should not be used since they run counter to the 'zero defects' ideal, and can lead to a view that some poor quality is 'acceptable' or 'inevitable'. There is a measure of truth in this view, but the fact remains that many organisations still make use of sampling inspection, especiallly in non-critical situations, where the cost of a proportion of reject-quality material getting through to the manufacturing process is not great.

Suggestions for further work

If a package such as MINITAB is available, generation of random samples from various distributions can enhance understanding of the ideas of this chapter. For instance, the Poisson approximation to the Binomial can be vividly illustrated by plotting histograms, as can the way in which Binomial and Poisson both approach normality, as n and the mean respectively tend to infinity.

More able students are likely to want to know how we can be sure that a variable does follow a Normal distribution. Plotting a sample – perhaps a height or weight distribution for a large class – on Normal probability paper can form a useful exercise. Looking at histograms of some computer-generated random samples can also illustrate how unreliable 'looking at the graph' can be as a means of assessing normality. MINITAB's NSCORES command simplifies the plotting of normal scores (though few students really understand the underlying mechanism). If the sample values are in C1, the NSCORES C1 C2 places the corresponding Normal scores in C2. PLOT C1 C2 should then yield an approximate straight line if the sample is Normal.

Chapter 10
SAMPLING AND INFERENCE

Outline content

This chapter covers:
- the concept of the sampling distribution of a statistic;
- the form of the sampling distributions for large sample means and percentages, with their standard errors;
- the concept of a confidence interval, and the procedures for computing such intervals;
- the question of the sample size required to achieve a given level of accuracy in an estimate.

Teaching this material

As with basic probability theory, many students will find this material conceptually demanding. Of course, it is possible to teach students to construct confidence intervals, and later to carry out significance tests, without trying to impart a real understanding of what is going on – but it is hardly pedagogically satisfactory to do so. Moreover, if students are to acquire an understanding of, for example, the idea of a p-value in a significance test, then they need to have a good grasp of the sampling distribution concept.

If possible, I like to approach the material informally first, from two angles. One is the exploitation of 'common sense' – the fact that most people understand intuitively that not all samples will exactly represent the population from which they are taken, that larger samples will in some way be 'more reliable' than small samples, and that a population parameter will be 'round about' the value obtained from a sample. From this follows the view that all we are doing in studying sampling theory is setting this common sense on a more quantified footing.

The second line of approach is via 'simulation'. The Central Limit Theorem, for example, can be conveyed clearly by generation of creasingly large random samples from a Normal, Uniform, Exponential, etc., distribution, and plotting of the sample means. A sampling distribution of percentages, too, can be produced by random sample generation from Bernoulli distribution. If there is time, a 'hand' rather than computerised experiment may well carry even more weight; one such is outlined in Question 10 of the practical exercises.

Solutions to the exercises

1 The proportion in the sample is 208/400 = 52 per cent.

   We can use this as an approximation to the population proportion, so that standard error = STEP =

$$\sqrt{(52 \times 48)/400} = 2.50$$

Thus:

p(population proportion actually greater than 50 per cent) =
$p(z \geq -2/2.5)$ =
$p(z \geq -0.8)$ =
$1 - p(z \leq -0.8)$ =
$1 - 0.2119 = 0.7881$.

Really what we are working out here is a sort of one-sided confidence interval – we are 79 per cent confident that the population value is in the interval 50 per cent to 100 per cent.

The sample would need to be a simple random sample for the argument to hold in this form – an unlikely occurrence in the case of a real pre-election survey, as these are generally carefully stratified. A discussion of the opinion polls prior to the April '92 General Election, and their lack of success in predicting the outcome, could fruitfully be introduced here.

2 Proportions again: 15/40 = 37.5 per cent
   STEP = $\div(37.5 \times 62.5/40) = 7.65$

   (a) 95 per cent interval is roughly 37.5 per cent ±

        2 x 7.65 per cent, which is 22.19 per cent to 52.81 per cent – a large interval reflecting the uncertainty inherent in the small sample size.

   (b) A 99 per cent interval is 37.5 ± 2.58 × 7.65 = 17.76 per cent to 57.24 per cent. For higher confidence we need a wider interval.

3 21/75 = 28 per cent can tell the difference, so 72 per cent can't. To   calculate STEP here we should use the population percentage, which is   given as 80 per cent. This makes STEP 4.62 per cent, and so p(sample of 75 contains 72 per cent or less who can't tell the difference) =
   $p(z < (72 - 80)/4.62) = p(z < 1.73) = 0.0418$.

The interpretation of this is that the 75 in the sample are a pretty unusual group if the manufacturer's statement is correct. Thus, we might doubt the claim when faced with this evidence.

This is, of course, really a hypothesis test, though students should be able to think their way through it without knowing the formal approach. Some will object that we should not use the 80 per cent figure in calculating STEP because 'it may not be true'. The point that needs emphasising in response is that we are looking at the probability that a hypothetical population with 80 per cent *could* lead to a sample such as we have found.

4 STEM = $0.4/\sqrt{160} = 0.05$, so 95 per cent interval is roughly 5.4 to 5.6 minutes. It can't be said too often that what this means is that if we were to make lots of estimates in this way using different samples, then 95 per cent of the interval would indeed contain the population mean. The population mean itself, of course, being determinate, either does or does not fall in one particular interval.

5 It will probably take some nudging to elicit from students the fact that STEP takes its greatest value for a given sample size when p = 50 per cent. So if we have no prior idea of the value of p, we should use 50 per cent to be on the safe side in the

sense of getting a large enough sample.

STEP = $\sqrt{(50 \times 50/n)}$, and we want the 99 per cent confidence range to be equal to 1 per cent Thus our 2.58 STEP = 1, STEP = 0.388, and so $\sqrt{(50 \times 50/n)}$ = 0.388, from which n is about 16,600.

Some students will find the manipulation of the algebra in this argument a bit tricky; there is also scope for confusion of the 'does the 1 per cent have anything to do with the 99 per cent?' kind. The point needs to be made that to get the two sides of the equation for determining n, we use two independent facts:

(a) the required accuracy is 1 per cent, and
(b) the confidence level is 99 per cent.

The size of the sample may surprise some students – for a high degree of accuracy and confidence from sampling a proportion, big samples will be required. For sampling of measured variables, which is more discriminating, one can 'get away with' generally smaller samples.

6 (a) The 99 per cent confidence interval is 423 +/– 2.58 × 115/$\sqrt{65}$ = £386.20 to £459.80. The wide range of this estimate is due, first to the fact that 65 is quite a small sample, and second, to the fairly large s.d. of the population. It is worth emphasising that we are not claiming that all customers spend within this range – the range of individual spending will be much wider – but that the average expenditure for the whole population falls in the range.

(b) To get an estimate to within £25, with the same level of confidence and the same s.d., we would need 2.58 × 115/$\sqrt{n}$ = 25, when n = 141 approximately. So a futher 76 people would need to be questioned. The sample size is just over twice what it was in part (a), for a reduction of just over £11 in the error margin.

7 (a) STEP = $\sqrt{(10 \times 90/100)}$ = 3% and the 95 per cent confidence interval will be roughly 6 per cent in width.

(b) When n = 400, STEP = 1.5%; when n = 900 STEP = 1% and when n= 1600, STEP = 0.75%.

(c) The graph is of course a hyperbola, since STEP decreases like 1$\sqrt{n}$. It is perhaps easier to see the implications of this by noting that, for a doubling of the accuracy of estimates we need to quadruple the size of the sample.

(d) The point here is that an increase of the sample size from 100 to 400 gives a very substantial improvement in accuracy in absolute terms, as we saw above – STEP reducing 3 per cent to 1.5 per cent. But by the time we get to sample sizes of 1,000 or more, the improvements in absolute accuracy are not nearly so impressive; a sample size of 1,000 with a population percentage around 10 will give a standard error of less than 1 per cent. Since sampling can be expensive – for instance, when interviewing is involved – it is often simply not cost-effective to obtain very large samples, the accuracy obtained from a smaller sample being adequate.

It should be emphasized to students that all this applies only to samples from very large populations. When the sample constitutes a substantial proportion of the entire population. The finite population correction, by reducing the standard error, gives results perhaps more in line with the intuitive belief that 'the bigger the sample the better'.

8–12 The danger with any sampling investigation such as the ones suggested here is that the results obtained in a particular case may not agree with theory – so the teacher needs to be good at convincing students that this doesn't invalidate the theory, but in fact substantiates what has been said about sampling variations. Of course, if several groups are carrying out the same exercise, there should be a better spread of results.

13 (a) The mean age of males in the group is 31.75 years, with standard deviation 3.73. Since the sample size on which this figure is based is 88 (not 143, it should be noted), this gives a standard error of 0.40, and consequently a 95 per cent confidence interval of 30.97 to 32.52 years.

If MINITAB is being used, then the standard error can be obtained directly using the DESCRIBE function, with subcommand BY to separate out males from females.

(b) The proportion of overseas students in the sample is 28.67 per cent, giving a standard error of percentage of 7.41 per cent, and a confidence interval of 21.26 per cent to 36.08 per cent. It is worth pointing out that this interval is quite wide due to the relatively small size of the sample.

Suggestions for further work

Questions 8–12 of the practical exercises provide some ideas for experimental work in this area. The results from the survey carried out as part of the work in Chapter 3 can be revisited here, and point estimates obtained there can be extended to confidence intervals. There are often other areas of course work (e.g. marketing) which engage in work where the methods of this chapter can have an input.

Finally, it is very easy for the routine of constructing a confidence interval to become a sort of thought-free process, without comprehension of what is actually going on. Asking questions such as, 'How would you answer an engineer who says 'What percentage confidence can I have in this experimental result?' can be illuminating – if sometimes depressing.

Chapter 11
HYPOTHESIS TESTING

Outline content

This chapter covers:
- testing of hypotheses on large sample proportions using a Normal approximation to Binomial;
- *z*-tests of hypotheses on large sample means;
- *t*-tests of hypotheses on means of small samples from Normal populations;
- use of the chi-squared test for goodness-of-fit testing and for association in contingency tables.

Teaching this material

The approach to hypothesis testing used in this chapter differs from that used in many texts. Rather than advocating the computation of a z-value which is then compared with some critical value in order to reach a decision, the method I use involves the calculation of an acceptance interval, and the decision rule is 'do not reject the NH if the sample value lies in the interval'. I believe that this approach encourages students to think more carefully about the meaning of the decision, as well as making more sense of the idea of type I and type II errors. However, I do give a brief coverage of the more usual method.

I also make only brief mention of one-tailed tests, but any student who has grasped the hypothesis testing logic should have no difficulty in applying it in a one-tailed situation when required.

Whatever method is adopted, the major difficulty in teaching hypothesis testing is to avoid the reduction of the method to a 'recipe'. Of course, students *like* recipes, and indeed I have given a summarised procedure for hypothesis testing on pp. 221–4 of *Quantitative Approaches in Business Studies* which looks very much like one! But particularly with the increasing use of computer packages which quote the *p*-value of a test as part of the standard output, it is important for anyone using hypothesis tests to have a clear understanding of the logical basis of the process.

Another difficulty encountered is confusion at the apparent variety of tests. Again, this can to some extent be minimised by an appreciation that the underlying argument is the same in all cases – only the test statistic being used varies.

The third problem area is formulation of the null hypothesis. This is a step which students frequently omit, leading to confusion as to what has actually been demonstrated at the end of the test procedure. Descriptions like that found in a solution manual for an external examining body – 'the null hypothesis is the one you hope to reject' – do not help! There are many ways of phrasing an NH, but perhaps stressing the 'no difference' or 'nothing's changed' aspect is most useful. Furthermore, it is the value of the parameter (mean, percentage, etc.) postulated by the null hypothesis which is then placed in the centre of the acceptance interval – NOT the sample value, another popular error.

One particular point which needs emphasis is that it is not merely the size of a sample which determines whether a z or t-test is appropriate – the crucial fact, given Normality of the parent population, is whether or not the population variance is known.

The term 'significant' is another unfortunate instance of a word which has a different meaning in statistics from its colloquial one. A point worth making – particularly in teaching students who one hopes will use these ideas in an applied context – is that significant in the statistical sense does not necessarily mean 'important' or 'meaningful'. All we claim when we state that a result is significant is that the probability that it could have arisen by chance from the null hypothesis population is only 5 per cent (or 1 per cent, or whatever).

Finally, the wording of conclusions is important. The one-word answer 'sig' or 'not sig' gets few marks from me! Likewise, statements such as 'we have proved that there is no difference' are definitely to be discouraged.

As with confidence intervals, perhaps the best way in to this area is via 'commonsense' arguments: something which varies only a bit from what you expected doesn't cause you any worries; if you get a result *very* different from what you expected, you begin to think that perhaps your expectation was not right after all. The formal procedure of hypothesis testing simply puts this intuitive argument on a more quantified basis.

A note on the worksheet CHI.XLS

This worksheet uses the data from the cross-tabulation of 'time on job' against 'improvement' (p. 241 of the text) to illustrate the computation of expected frequencies and of the chi-squared statistic. However, in order to facilitate use of the worksheet for larger contingency tables, the table for computation of chi-squared does not reference the cells in the contingency table; instead, the relevant values of O and E have simply been transferred manually. As with the other worksheets, the major value to students is in exploring the structure of the worksheet and relating it to the process of computation as they have carried it out by hand; it can then be used to relieve the computational effort in other similar problems.

Solutions to the exercises

1 This is a large sample, with $n = 100$.

   NH: This factory has the same mean as the rest, i.e. mean for population at factory = 110.

   AH: Mean for factory is different from £110.

   As means are involved, we use:

   STEM = $7.50/\sqrt{100}$ = 0.75.

   The acceptance interval then becomes $110 \pm 2 \times 0.75$, using 5 per cent significance.

   The sample value of £108 falls outside this interval, and so we conclude that the sample does provide evidence that workers at this factory differ from the rest of the industry – the difference is significant at the 5 per cent level.

(This question provides an opportunity to discuss the effect of finite populations on the theory. The argument, as it stands, only applies if the workforce at the factory is considerably larger – ten times is a rule of thumb sometimes applied – than the sample of 100.)

2 Here $n = 80$, and we need STEP.

NH: proportion is still 40 per cent

AH: proportion has changed. (No doubt marketing people would like to test a 1-tailed alternative here!)

STEP = $\sqrt{(40 \times 60/80)} = 5.48$

The acceptance interval is $40 \pm 2.58 \times 5.48$ (2.58 for 1 per cent sig.) = 25.86 per cent to 54.14 per cent. Our sample contained $41/80 = 51.25$ per cent.

As this lies in the interval, we cannot reject the NH – the sample provides no grounds for concluding that the promotion has changed the proportion stocking the product (at the 1 per cent significance level).

(Some students may be tempted here to try to work with numbers rather than percentages – the fact that the standard error formula for STEP is based on percentages needs to be emphasised.)

3 Chi-squared for a contingency table, thus:

	Male	*Female*	*Total*
Union	97(90)	53(60)	150
Non-union	23(30)	27(20)	50
Total	120	80	200

Expected frequencies are shown in brackets. They are calculated thus:

NH is that there is no association between gender and unionisation.

If this is true, then the overall proportion of 25 per cent non-union should be equally reflected among men and women. So, for example, of 120 men we would expect 30 to be non-union. Because the table has only one degree of freedom, once this figure has been calculated all the other expected frequencies follow.

Chi-squared can then be computed as:

$\Sigma\{|O - E| - 0.5\}^2/E = 4.69$ (using Yates' correction).

The value of chi-squared for 1 degree of freedom and 5 per cent significance is 3.841. As our chi-squared is greater than this, we reject the null hypothesis and conclude that there is evidence of an association between gender and unionisation, significant at the 5 per cent level.

46

4 Null hypothesis: there is no association between inspectors and levels of rejects.

	Accepted	Rejected	Total
A	75(75)	15(15)	90
B	83(85)	19(17)	102
C	92(90)	16(18)	108
Total	250	50	300

Chi-squared = 0.55.

There are two degrees of freedom, so the critical value of chi-squared at the 5 per cent level is 5.991.

There are no grounds for concluding that the inspectors differ in the proportion of items they reject.

5 Null hypothesis: the proportions found in the sample are consistent with the theory.

	Fair	Red	Dark	Total
Observed	60	19	66	150
Expected	60	15	75	150

Chi-squared = 2.56

There are two degrees of freedom (number of categories − 1), so the critical value of chi-squared is 5.991 (5 per cent sig.). Our chi-squared fails to reach this level, so we have no grounds for doubting the theory.

6 (a) STEM = $5.2/\sqrt{83}$ = 0.57, so we can estimate the mean number of journeys for the whole population with 95 per cent confidence to be $14 \pm 2 \times 0.57$, or about 12.86 to 15.14 journeys.

   (b) This requires a hypothesis test, the null hypothesis being that there has been no change in the proportion using the service for travel to work only, i.e. this proportion is still 48 per cent.

   STEP = $\sqrt{(48 \times 52/83)}$ = 5.48%, so that 95 per cent of samples of 83 per cent would be expected to have percentages in the range $48 \pm 2 \times 5.48$ or about 37 to 59 per cent. The actual percentage in this sample is 37/83 = 44.6%, which is well within this range, so there is no evidence to support the hypothesis that the proportion has changed, at the 5 per cent level of significance.

   (c) This calls for a chi-squared test of the null hypothesis 'no assoication between satisfaction and reasons'. The calculation is as shown on p. 48:

Obs	Exp	$(O-E)^2/E$
11	16.49	1.83
11	7.13	2.10
15	13.37	0.20
26	20.51	1.47
5	8.87	1.69
15	16.63	0.16
Chi-squared		7.44

The critical value of chi-squared with 2 degrees of freedom at 5 per cent significance is 5.99 so the test indicates a significant association. From inspection of the table it seems that those who use the service for work purposes only are less satisfied than might be expected, those who use it for leisure are more satisfied.

The main difficulty students encounter with this question is likely to be 'What am I supposed to do here?', since, unlike most other problems encountered so far, there is no indication as to whether a hypothesis test, an estimate or some other computation is required. Students should also be encouraged to interpret the results of their tests in practical terms – for example, the result in part (c) might encourage the bus company to investigate why travellers to work are less satisfied with its service, but since the test was carried out at the 5 per cent level there is a 5 per cent chance that a type! error has been made, in which case the company could spend quite a lot of effort and money pursuing a conclusion which is in fact incorrect.

9 The means and standard deviations of the male and female ages are as follows:

	Female	Male
Mean	34.36	31.75
S.D.	4.95	3.74

If we are prepared to assume that the two samples come from populations with a common variance as well as a common mean, then the estimate of the population variance obtained by pooling the samples is 18.03 (= $[55 \times 4.95^2 + 88 \times 3.74^2]/143$) so that the pooled s.d. is 4.24.

Then the standard error of the difference in means will be

$$4.24 \times \text{sqrt}(1/55 + 1/88) = 0.73.$$

Since we are looking for a difference in either direction, the appropriate null hypothesis is that population mean age for females is equal to that for males. The test statistic then becomes

$$z = (34.36 - 31.75)/0.73 = 3.58,$$

and so the null hypothesis can be rejected at the 1 per cent level.

Much the same results can be obtained by using the MINITAB command TWOT with subcommand POOLED, as shown on p. 49.

```
MTB > twot c1 c3;
SUBC> pooled.
```

TWOSAMPLE T FOR AGE

GENDER	N	MEAN	STDEV	SE MEAN
1	88	31.75	3.74	0.40
0	55	34.36	4.95	0.67

95 PCT CI FOR MU 1- MU O: (−4.06, −1.17)

TTEST MU 1 = MU O (VS NE): T= −3.58 P=0.0005 DF= 141

POOLED STDEV =   4.24

It is worth exploring this question a little further, since in fact the difference in age between males and females is restricted to the home students, there being no significant difference for the overseas group; performing the analysis on both groups combined obscures this fact. When the groups are separated, the difference for the home students shows up as even more highly significant.

10 Here STEM = $0.8/\sqrt{40}$ = 0.13. If we are concerned only about a decline in standards, then a 1-sided test is appropriate. The significance level used will determine how often we get a 'false alarm' – that is, how often we conclude that there is a decline when in fact we are simply seeing normal sampling variation consistent with the established standard. A significance level of 1 per cent will mean this occurs, on average, only once in 100 months; an interesting discussion can take place around the 'best' level to use, linking in to the concept of type 1 and type 2 errors. Taking the 1 per cent level, we can conclude that a sample with a mean more than 2.33 standard errors above 5.2 is a cause for concern – that is, it would cause us to reject the null hypothesis of no decline in standards. This leads to a limit of 5.2 + 2.33 × 0.13 = 5.50 days.

Students can then be led towards the control chart ideas covered in the next chapter by the reflection that no-one wants to be performing hypothesis tests once a month if they can help it, so an automated way of carrying out the test – perhaps by plotting the means of samples on a chart with a 'danger limit' marked at 5.50 – is called for. The point needs to be stressed at this stage that it is the means, *not* individual values, which are being monitored – failure to grasp this can lead to much confusion later.

Suggestions for further work

More able students may well get more insight into the process of hypothesis testing through a fuller discussion of the Type I/Type II Error question, perhaps in conjunction with the idea of an Operating Characteristic for a test, and the related concept of the power of the test. This can lead to discussion of how a suitable significance level (and, where necessary, a beta-level – risk of making a type II error) should be decided.

However, for most students a good deal of practice on fairly routine testing examples will be required, especially in terms of deciding what distribution (*t*, Normal, or chi-squared) is involved, and which standard error (STEM, STEP, STEDM) should be used.

Chapter 12
QUALITY IMPROVEMENT

Outline content

This chapter covers:
- **the seven tools of quality improvement (checksheets, Pareto charts, cause-and-effect diagrams, histograms, stratification, scatterplots and control charts);**
- **the construction and interpretation of control charts for means, ranges and attribute data;**
- **process capability and capability indices;**
- **sampling inspection schemes.**

Teaching this material

In previous editions of the book I had decided not to include material on Quality Improvement, being of the opinion that the statistical aspects of this topic were best examined in the wider context of a managerial treatment of the topic. However, discussion with colleagues and with students has convinced me that there is a place for an explanation of the role of sampling and inference in the quality improvement process, though clearly it is still important for students to receive parallel input on aspects such as the behavioural and operations management implications of TQM if they are to have a rounded picture of the strength of the methods.

There is a tendency for undergraduate students in particular to undervalue the simpler techniques such as cause-and-effect diagrams and histograms, regarding them as rather trivial. I have found it effective to ask tutorial groups to choose some aspect of their course which they regard as 'a quality problem' (slow return of marked work, for example!) and to ask them to carry out a brainstorm on possible causes of the problem, then use the tools to structure their thinking and work towards potential solutions. This usually gains their attention.

With postgraduates the problem tends to be somewhat different; many of them will now come from a service rather than a manufacturing background, and really good cases of service-oriented application of the ideas are still in short supply – one gets rather tired of monitoring the number of times a telephone rings before it is answered as a benchmark of customer service. Again, getting students to produce examples from their own experience where the methods might be appropriate is usually the best way of demonstrating the usefulness of the methods.

Solutions to the exercises

1 The two versions of the Pareto are shown on pages 470 and 471 of the book. They demonstrate how the Pareto by frequency is dominated by:

2 (a) Using the 60 per cent figure, the value of STEP becomes $\sqrt{(60 \times 40/50)}$ = 6.93%, and so the 3 STEP limits would run from 39.21 per cent to 80.79 per cent – a very wide range, due to the small samples being used.

(b) With the target figure of 80 per cent, STEP becomes $\sqrt{(80 \times 20/50}$ = 5.65%, and the limits move to 63.05 per cent to 96. 95 per cent. Although the sample size is the same, the range here is somewhat smaller due to the higher target percentage being used.

(c) If the current overall percentage is 60 per cent, it would be very unwise to move immediately to the limits based on the target figure, as a very large proportion of samples would inevitably fall below the lower limit. This could be demoralising for staff, and unless stapes are taken to raise the level of performance, the failures are inevitable. It would be better to act to raise the proportion, leaving the limits based on the current 60 per cent figure until the charts show definite evidence of improvement. New limits could then be recalculated based on the new overall figure, and the process repeated. In this way, gradual improvement can be achieved without creating large numbers of 'failing' samples.

3 The process capability index C_p in this case is $3/(6 \times 0.52)$ or 0.96. The fact that it is below 1 suggests that the process cannot meet its specifications, though since C_p is so close to 1, we might assume that the proportion out-of-spec will not be too great.

However, when C_{pk} is calculated, we obtain C_{pk} = min$[(24.5 - 22.88)/(33 \times 52)$, $(22.88 - 21.5)/(3 \times 0.52)]$ = min$[1.04, 0.88]$ = 0.88, showing that because of poor centring of the process, the problem is in fact more serious – the process mean is too close to the lower specification limit.

The proportion of reject items which will be produced can be calculated from the Normal distribution as indicated in Fig. 12.1:

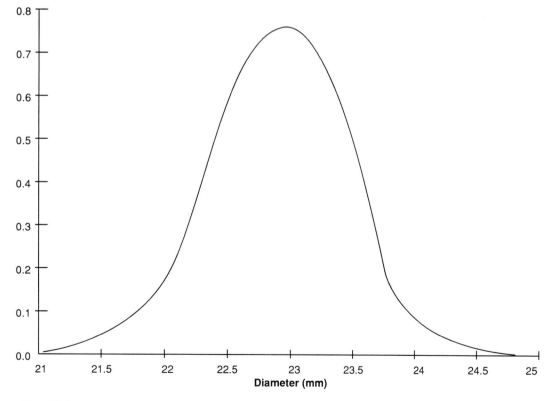

Fig. 12.1

51

At the upper end, z = 3.12, giving a proportion of 0.00097 (using the nearest figure from the table in Appendix 5) or more accurately 0.000904 (using the NORMSDIST function in Excel). At the lower end we have z = 2.65, whence the proportion is 0.00402. The total proportion is thus about 0.0049 or nearly half a percent, which could be quite serious in a large volume of production – almost one head piece in 200 will be out-of-spec.

If the process can be better centred, so that the mean is exactly 23 mm as required, then the proportion out-of-spec will reduce. z at each end will then be 1.5/0.52 or 2.88, so the overall proportion is 2 × 0.00199 = approximately 0.4%. A y improvement beyond this will have to be produced by a reduction in the standard deviation – perhaps by training workers to operate machines more accurately, or by purchasing better equipment. Either of these alternatives could, of course, be expensive, and needs to be weighed up against the cost of rejects under the present system.

4 The mean of the sample means for the first twenty samples is 27.00739, and the mean range is 1.50919. Since the samples are of size 5, Table XII shows that the relevant constant for the means chart is 0.58, and so the limits become 27.00739 ± 0.58 × 1.50919 or 26.1321 to 27.8827, rounding to 4 d.p.

For the range chart, the constants are 0 and 2.11, so the lower limit is zero and the upper 2.11 × 1.50919 = 3.1844 to 4 d.p.

When the charts are plotted, there are no points outside the limits, and no discernible patterns which would give rise for concern, so it would appear that the process is in a state of statistical control.

It needs to be emphasised to students that the limits plotted have nothing whatsoever to do with any specification limits on the process – in this case we are not even told what the limits on the specification of the foot joint are, and it is entirely possible that the process, while in statistical control, is producing large amounts of out-of-spec material – we simply cannot tell. All we know from the charts is that there have been, in the course of the 40 samples given, no evident special cause variations needing investigation.

5 (a) This situation calls for a c-chart based on the Poisson distribution. With a mean of 5.2, tables show that the probability of 11 or more shut-downs in a week is 0.0177, while the probability of 12 or more is 0.0073. If a threshold of 1 in 100 has been set, then the limit should be placed between 11 and 12, so that 12 or more shutdowns in a week would be regarded as evidence of a deterioration in the process.

   (b) Since probability of 1 or more shutdowns is 0.9945, the probability of no shutdowns is 0.0055. Probability of 2 or more is 0.9658, so probability of 1 or none is 0.0342. The limit should thus be placed between 0 and 1; only a week with no shutdowns would indicate a significant improvement.

      The above computations are based on the assumption that the occurrence of shutdowns is a random event, but in practice it a large amount of data is available one would wish to examine it for possible seasonal patterns, trends, etc, before applying this rather simple-minded thinking.

6 (a) (i) This is a binomial situation with n = 10, p = 0.05.
p(reject) = p(one or more defectives) = 0.4013

(ii) When p = 0.1, p(reject) = 0.6513.

(iii) When p = 0.2, p(reject) = 0.8926.

(b) The operating characteristic is thus as shown in Fig. 12.2

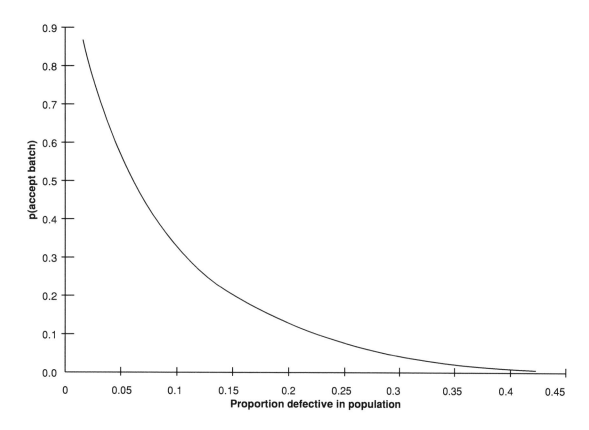

Fig. 12.2

This scheme is not a very effective one, since it permits over 10 per cent of very poor-quality batches (20 per cent defective) to get through inspection. In practice a larger sample would be required for better discrimination. Using probabilities obtained from MINITAB or Excel, it is possible for students to construct operating characteristics for other schemes; for example, that for n = 30, with rejection if more than 1 defective is found, is as shown in Fig. 12.3 overleaf.

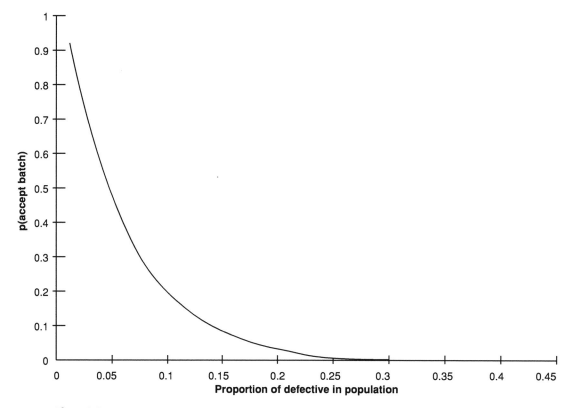

Fig. 12.3

Normally the producer's risk (probability of rejecting an 'acceptable' batch) and the consumer's risk (probability of accepting a 'really unacceptable' batch) would be decided by negotiation between supplier and customer, and then a scheme would be chosen which passes as close as possible to the two points defined by these risks. Since the situation is discrete it will not, of course, generally be possible to find a scheme giving precisely the risks specified.

(c) With p = 0.05, we have seen that p(reject) under this scheme is 0.4013. So about 40 of the 100 batches will be rejected – that's 40 × 5000 or 200,000 zips. Of these, on average 95 per cent or 190,000 would be satisfactory. The inspection scheme thus results in the return of a good deal of perfectly acceptable material – not a very desirable state of affairs.

Chapter 13
CORRELATION

Outline content

This chapter covers:
- calculation and interpretation of Pearson's product-moment correlation coefficient;
- calculation and interpretation of Spearman's rank correlation coefficient.

Teaching this material

Correlation is a topic on which it is usually relatively easy to motivate students – the urge to find out 'if there's a connection' seems to be universal.

I think that even with students at an elementary level, it is worth discussing the question of the significance of the coefficient – otherwise one has to fall back on a purely subjective interpretation of 'closeness to one'. Again, the fact that as sample size increases, smaller values of r are regarded as significant can be tied to the commonsense fact that with only two points one would always have perfect correlation, so clearly a two-point sample doesn't convey any information at all.

Solutions to the exercises

1 $\Sigma d^2 = 16$, so $r_{rank} = 0.903$, indicating a fair degree of consistency (with rank correlation we should not use the significance table for r).

2 $\Sigma d^2 = 4.5$, giving $r_{rank} = 0.95$. This is consistent with the statement, though of course it does not *prove* that the oil content is causing the better flavour.

   (The tying values of 32 must be ranked 1.5 and 1.5, as they would have ranks 1 and 2 if they differed.)

   If the ranking is done in the reverse direction, the only change is in the sign of the coefficient, though the calculation looks quite different.

3 With age = x, consumption = y, we have:

   (a) $\Sigma o = 47$, $\Sigma x^2 = 413$, $\Sigma y = 32$, $\Sigma y^2 = 210$, $\Sigma xy = 292$.
        So $s_x = 2.73$, $s_y = 2.56$, covariance = 6.89, and $r = 0.99$.

   (b) $\Sigma o = 104$, $\Sigma x^2 = 1538$, $\Sigma y = 62$, $\Sigma y^2 = 512$, $\Sigma xy = 868$.
        So $s_x = 6.1$, $s_y = 3.07$, covariance = 77.72, and $r = 0.90$.

   The explanation of the difference is that as the pig gets older, its weight increases less rapidly. What appears as a good linear relationship over the first year of its life is therefore no longer so clearly linear when two years are considered.

4 The coefficient is 0.8 as before – scaling the two variables by different factors does not affect the result.

5 The *x*-values have been scaled to $2x + 10$, and the *y*'s to $3y - 100$ – again the value of the coefficient does not alter. So we can simplify data by subtracting or adding, multiplying or dividing by constant amounts, without altering the results of correlation calculations.

6 (a) The correlation for all ten employees is –0.43. The negative value should surprise any student who has thought about the data at all – as people get older, they are normally paid more.

(b) The scattergraph is as shown in Fig. 13.1.

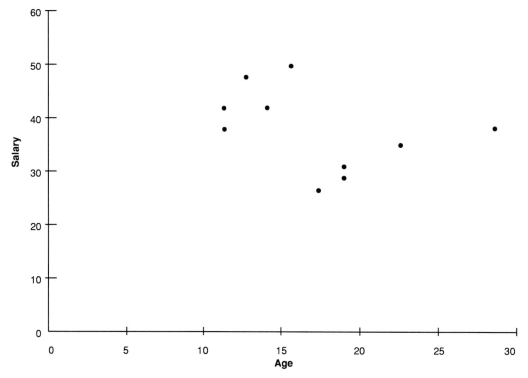

Fig. 13.1

This makes it clear that actually the sample contained two distinct groups of workers. In each group, there is the expected positive correlation between age and salary, but one group is generally older and less well-paid than the other. It is the combination of the two groups which has given rise, misleadingly, to the apparent negative relationship. The two groups should really be analysed separately, although the samples are then rather small; it might be advisable to gather more data on each group.

The moral of this question is that it is *always* worth plotting a scattergraph before proceeding to further analysis – and thinking about what it shows!

7 Time-series data is very often selected by students for this kind of exercise, and while I do not consider it appropriate in a course at this level to go into details of the underlying conditions for the correlation and regression models (independence, normality, etc.), I think it is important to point out the likelihood of serial correlation in economic and other time series, leading to a 'non-random scatter' of points

56

around any fitted line. Moreover, put crudely, any two sets of data which increase over time will give some kind of positive correlation; so we need to discuss whether it might be better to correlate year-on-year per cent changes rather than absolute figures. The need to deflate data influenced by inflation can also be mentioned, linking back to the ideas of Chapter 7.

8   The results of the analysis are as shown; ptakings, pflspace denote the values of the takings and floorspace variables for the precinct branches, and stakings, sflspace for the street branches.

Correlation of TAKINGS and FLSPACE = 0.432

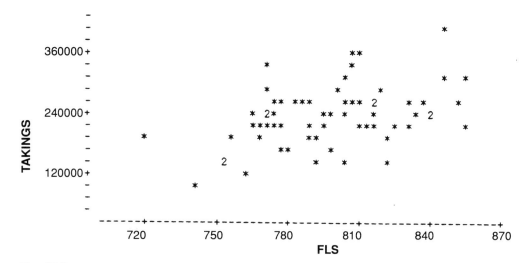

Fig. 13.2

Correlation of takings and pflspace = 294

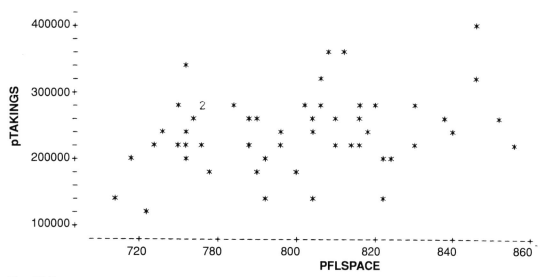

Fig. 13.3

The correlation coefficient for the 'street' branches is 0.736, as against 0.294 for the 'precinct' branches. However, we need to consult tables of the significance of these figures in order to draw fair conclusions, since the corresponding degrees of freedom (9 and 51 respectively) are very different. When this is done, we see that the 'street' results are just significant at the 1 per cent level, whereas the 'precinct' results only reach the 5 per cent level. It is debatable whether the analysis of the combined results is actually worth carrying out, since the features of the separate groups may be obscured – just as with the 'difference of ages' test on the STUD data in the previous chapter.

Correlation of stakings and sflspace = 0.736

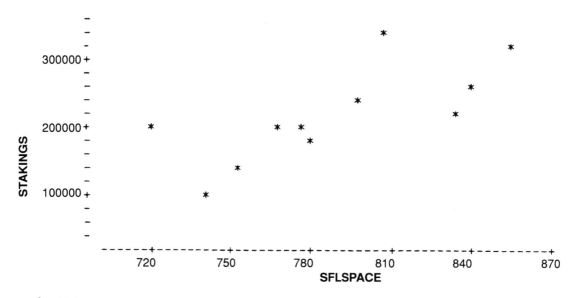

Fig. 13.4

Suggestions for further work

This is another area where it is easy to find published data which can be investigated for correlations. However, if students are given a free hand in the collection of data then a number of points need to be emphasised:

1 Time-series data has particular problems – two sets of data both of which exhibit an increasing trend over time (e.g. financial figures affected by inflation) may produce a 'good' correlation which means little in practice. Indexing data, deflating it, or correlating year-on-year changes provide possible ways around this problem. Alternatively, use other kinds of cross-sectional data (e.g. regional).

2 The fact that a significant correlation does not imply a *causal* relationship cannot be too strongly stressed – the causal mechanisms with real data may be complex.

Chapter 14
LINE FITTING

Outline content

This chapter covers:
- **the fitting and use of least-squares regression lines;**
- **the construction and applications of semi-log graphs.**

Teaching this material

It is difficult to know precisely where to draw the boundaries when teaching regression. This edition of *Quantitative Approaches* emphasizes the use of MINITAB and Excel and includes a mention of analysis of variance, as well as the testing of regression coefficients. However, I have not given details of conditions for validity of the regression model, residual plotting, etc.; for most students at this level it remains more important to stress the interpretation of the regression equation, with its consequent potential hazards (extrapolation, the presence of 'lurking' variables, and so on).

For the weaker student the concepts involved in plotting and interpreting a linear equation may be a stumbling block. I have found that an emphasis on the interpretation of the constant term and x-coefficient in the practical terms of the problem is helpful here – many students for whom 'intercept' is a foreign notion can easily grasp the idea of 'this is the level of sales when there's no advertising', etc.

As far as semi-log graphs are concerned, the word 'log' may be alarming to students who have a foggy recollection of 'doing logs' from school days. Rather than attempting to explain the connection with logs, I find it preferable to get students to examine the printed log scale on a sheet of semi-log paper, or on a computer-generated graph, and confirm for themselves that the distance from, say, 2 to 4 is the same as that from 4 to 8, etc. Most will then find it easy to see that increases by equal factors will produce straight lines on such a scale.

Solutions to the exercises

1 We should use the stronger linear relationship here, (i.e. the one based on only the first six points), since the value $x = 5$ months falls within this range. Using the values of s_x etc. computed in answer to exercise 3, Chapter 12, we find:

$$y - 5.33 = \{(0.99 \times 2.56)/2.73\}(x - 7.83)$$

i.e. $y = 0.92x - 1.87$ (slight discrepancies in answers may arise depending on how many figures have been retained in computations).

This gives a weight of 2.73 kg when $x = 5$.

2 Graphs of both costs and revenues are reasonably linear on semi-log paper, but as

the slope of the costs line is steeper than that for revenues, the latter will eventually be overtaken by the former if the present rates of increase continue. Depending on the precise position of the estimated lines, this will occur around year 14 or 15.

Of course, it is improbable that a firm would be faced with such a situation and fail to intervene before losses started to be made, so the assumption that the rates of change are constant is unlikely to be true in practice.

Students who are plotting the graph for this question need to be reminded that, in order to be able to extend the trend of the lines until they cross, a scale which will accommodate much more than the 5-year time-span given in the data will be needed. The question can also be neatly tackled via Excel, applying a log transformation to the cost and revenue figures, then fitting a regression line to get the exact form of the relationships, which can be extrapolated until costs > revenues.

3 It is certainly correct to say that the time spent with a company is strongly correlated with the number of sales – the correlation coefficient is significant at the 1 per cent level. However, the longest-serving salesman in the data set has done only just over four years, so using the relationship to predict sales for length of service, six years is a drastic extrapolation. The linear relationship in the initial months of service is likely to be due to a learning effect, but one would expect this gradually to level off as the salesman approaches saturation of his territory – or even to drop as he stops trying so hard!

The correlation between number of sales and mileage is virtually non-existent. There are two possible explanations for this:

(a) Other factors such as population density may affect a salesman's chance of making a sale – someone working in a densely populated area may not have to travel many miles in order to make a lot of sales.

(b) It is worth looking at the relationship with Adams excluded, since he appears to be an outlier with a very low level of sales and a very high mileage. Without him the correlation becomes 0.944, which is highly significant. The outlier status of Adams is clear from a scatterplot – one would need to follow up on why he is producing such high mileages to so little effect.

6 The output from MINITAB relating to the relevant regression analyses is as shown. Similar, though less complete, results may be obtained using Excel. General conclusions are that takings are much more strongly related to floorspace than to staff; in fact, the R-squared (adj) value is exactly the same for the two-predictor model as for the model with floorspace alone. This suggests that there is little value in incorporating the second variable. Students may query the negative sign of the staff variable in the two-predictor model, which suggests that stores with fewer staff have larger takings; however, since the coefficient is not significantly different from zero, the 95 per cent confidence interval, for example, will actually include both positive and negative values.

It is worth observing that, though the coefficient of floorspace in the bivariate model differs significantly from zero, the explanatory power of the model as indicated by R-squared or R-squared (adj) is still not very high, suggesting that there are other important influences on takings which have not been considered.

It can also be noted that the constant term is significantly different from zero, suggesting that the relationship has a negative intercept – not surprisingly, in the absence of any staff or shop area, there will be a loss.

The question concerning the inclusion of the location variable gives an opportunity to discuss the use of dummy variables in a regression model, though here in fact the relation with location is not significant.

The existence of a large number of outlets, and the possibility of exclusion of some of them might also be explored.

MTB > regress 'takings' on 1 'flspace'

The regression equation is

TAKINGS = –452202 + 863 FLSPACE

Predictor	Coef	Stdev	t-ratio	p
Constant	–452202	182788	–2.47	0.016
FLSPACE	862.8	229.0	3.77	0.000

s = 53728   R-sq = 18.6%   R-sq(adj) = 17.3%

Analysis of Variance

SOURCE	DF	SS	MS	F	p
Regression	1	40971251712	40971251712	14.19	0.000
Error	62	1.78975E+11	2886699008		
Total	63	2.19947E+11			

Unusual observations

Obs.	FLSPACE	TAKINGS	Fit	Stdev.fit	Residual	St.Resid
7	846	403668	277715	12958	12952	2.42R
14	771	330226	213006	9069	117219	2.21R
30	807	350925	244067	7052	106859	2.01R
37	719	191681	168142	19215	23539	0.47X
56	811	364151	247518	7383	116633	2.19R
57	821	149025	256146	8591	107121	–2.02R

R denotes an obs. with a large st. resid.
X denotes an obs. whose x value gives it large influence.

MTB > regress 'takings' on 1 'flspace'

The regression equation is

TAKINGS = 112512 + 5161 STAFF

Predictor	Coef	Stdev	t-ratio	p
Constant	112512	76176	1.48	0.145
STAFF	5161	3170	1.63	0.109

s = 58327   R-sq = 4.1%   R-sq(adj) = 2.6%

Analysis of Variance

SOURCE	DF	SS	MS	F	p
Regression	1	9017981952	9017081952	2.65	0.109
Error	62	2.10929E+11	3402074368		
Total	63	2.19947E+11			

Unusual observations

Obs.	STAFF	TAKINGS	Fit	Stdev.fit	Residual	St.Resid
7	26.0	403668	246689	9826	156979	2.73R
8	21.0	93625	220886	11787	−127261	−2.23R
37	18.0	191681	205404	20137	−13723	−0.25X
56	24.0	364151	236368	7295	127783	2.21R

R denotes an obs. with a large st. resid.

X denotes an obs. whose x value gives it large influence.

MTB > regress 'takings' on 2 'flspace' 'staff'

The regression equation is

TAKINGS = −521231 + 1066 FLSPACE −3091 STAFF

Predictor	Coef	Stdev	t-ratio	p
Constant	−521231	195554	−2.67	0.010
FLSPACE	1066.0	307.0	3.47	0.001
STAFF	−3891	3914	−0.99	0.324

s = 53733   R-sq = 19.9%   R-sq(adj) = 17.3%

Analysis of Variance

SOURCE	DF	SS	MS	F	p
Regression	2	4382350312	2191175056	7.59	0.001
Error	61	1.76123E+11	2886699008		
Total	63	2.19947E+11			

SOURCE	DF	SEQ SS
FLSPACE	1	40971251712
STAFF	1	2852248832

Unusual observations

Obs.	FLSPACE	TAKINGS	Fit	Stdev.fit	Residual	St.resid
7	846	403668	279465	13079	124203	2.38R
14	771	330226	218967	19873	11259	2.11R
30	807	350925	241781	7481	109145	2.05R
37	719	191681	175205	20489	16475	0.33X
50	804	135813	246364	8451	−110550	−2.08R
56	811	364151	249935	7774	114215	2.15R
57	821	149025	256705	8610	−107680	−2.03R
58	815	254657	269762	20457	−15105	−0.03X

R denotes an obs. with a large st. resid.

X denotes an obs. whose x value gives it large influence.

MTB > regress 'takings' on 3 'flspace' 'staff' 'location'

The regression equation is

TAKINGS = –486268 + 1047 FLSPACE –4033 STAFF –4246 LOCATION

Predictor	Coef	Stdev	t-ratio	p
Constant	–486268	201108	–2.42	0.019
FLSPACE	1047.4	308.9	3.39	0.001
STAFF	–4033	3931	–1/03	0.309
LOCATION	–14246	18061	–0.79	0.433

s = 53900   R-sq = 20.7%   R-sq(adj) = 16.8%

Analysis of Variance

SOURCE	DF	SS	MS	F	p
Regression	3	45631135744	15210378240	5.24	0.003
Error	60	1.7431E+11	2905257472		
Total	63	2.19947E+11			

SOURCE	DF	SEQ SS
FLSPACE	1	40971251712
STAFF	1	2852248832
LOCATION	1	1807635712

Unusual observations

Obs.	FLSPACE	TAKINGS	Fit	Stdev.fit	Residual	St.resid
7	846	403668	280716	13215	122952	2.35R
14	771	330226	222327	11709	107899	2.05R
30	807	350925	243901	7912	107024	2.01R
37	719	191681	165715	23815	25966	0.54X
50	804	135813	248824	9033	–113011	–2.13R
56	811	364151	252123	8277	112027	2.10R
57	821	149025	258564	8593	–109540	–2.06R

R denotes an obs. with a large st. resid.
X denotes an obs. whose x value gives it large influence.

Hints on the case study question

There is little point in attempting to forecast business enquiries since, as we saw in the case study problem to Chapter 12, the direct correlation in the same week is very low.

For the private enquiries, the regression equation is:

no of enquiries = 12.6 + 2.01 × no. of appearances

When there are 5 appearances, we would predict 22 or 23 enquiries and we would expect this prediction to be fairly reliable: (a) because there is a strong correlation, and (b) because 5 is comfortably within the range of the original data.

However, for 12 appearances, although we can go through the motions of obtaining a prediction (36 or 37 enquiries) we are extrapolating quite a long way; the linear relationship between appearances and enquiries may not hold up with such heavy advertising.

It might be worth pointing out that apparently with no advertising at all, a rate of 12 or 13 enquiries per week might be expected (presumably via personal recommendation, repeat business, etc.). Each appearance generates about two new enquiries. One would need to ask whether, when the enquiries are translated into firm bookings received, the advertising is really cost-effective.

Suggestions for further work

The exercise suggested for the previous chapter, based on students' own selection of published data for a correlation study, can be continued here, though even more warnings about careful interpretation of the results will be needed – especially with time-series data. If a suitable computer package is available, fitting a model with two independent variables may be interesting. In this case, too, with more able students one can explore the idea of using transformations ($1/x$ log x, etc.) to linearise a relationship, which ties in nicely with the semi-log graphs material of this chapter.

Chapter 15
TIME-SERIES AND EXPONENTIAL SMOOTHING

Outline content

This chapter covers:
- the definition of components which may be present in a time-series of data (trend, seasonal, cyclical and random variations);
- methods of decomposing a series into these elements using both additive and multiplicative models;
- the use of these models for forecasting, and criteria for their suitability with given data;
- the simple exponential smoothing model and its use.

Teaching this material

The major problem in dealing with forecasting methods is selecting the appropriate method for a given set of data. No real dataset is likely to be a perfect fit to any model and, since the book covers only the two most elementary methods, it is quite likely that some real datasets encountered by students will not be appropriate for the use of either model. So there is a need in teaching the material to stress the fact that we are building *models* of real data – then students should be able to go on to read about more complex models if necessary.

The use of a spreadsheet or a dedicated forecasting package is essential to cover this material effectively. Hand-calculation of the methods is both tedious and liable to error. A spreadsheet makes it particularly easy to try several values of the smoothing constant with one set of data, or to try both additive and multiplicative decomposition models.

There is plenty of published data which can form the basis of practice in this area, particularly where decomposition methods are concerned. In the Monthly Digest of Statistics, for example, we have sunshine and rainfall data on a monthly basis; passenger flights out of the UK on a quarterly basis; fishery catches; production of wheat, potatoes, etc.; the list could be continued. Most of these will yield at least a reasonable picture when analyzed by decomposition.

A note on the worksheets TS.XLS and ES.XLS

These two Excel worksheets are set up to automate the processes described in the chapter. TS.XLS carries out additive-model analysis of the pork-pie data on page 339, while ES.XLS does simple exponential smoothing on the beef sausage data from page 351. Both worksheets can be overwritten with other data, and extended to cover a wider range of time-periods, though TS.XLS is suitable only for data with a four-quarterly pattern. The value of the smoothing constant in ES.XLS may be changed, and a graph could be built up showing how the mean-square-error varies with alpha, thus suggesting an 'optimal' value for a given dataset. Columns could also be added to compute alternative goodness-of-fit measures, such as Mean Absolute Percentage Variation. TS.XLS could be further modified by the addition of columns to carry out multiplicative analysis, so that the two models' performance on a particular dataset can be compared in terms of their random/residual variations.

Solutions to the exercises

1 The graph in Fig. 15.1 makes it clear that the amplitude of the excursions around the trend is increasing as the trend itself increases. The full analysis of the data is shown in Table 15.1.

Multiplicative Model

Actual	Trend	Actual – Trend	Actual – Trend as % of trend	Forecast	Random Variation
22					
70	44	26	59.09	65.19	4.81
40	77	−37	−48.05	38.42	1.58
121	119	2	1.68	121.31	−0.31
196	134	62	46.27	198.55	−2.55
85	167	−82	−49.10	83.32	1.68
220	209	11	5.26	213.05	6.95
322	224	98	43.75	331.90	−9.90
130					

Period 1 seasonal	1.94
Period 2 seasonal	48.17
Period 3 seasonal	−50.11

Additive Model

Actual	Trend	Actual – Trend	Forecast	Random Variation
22				
70	44	26	103	−33
40	77	−37	14.5	25.5
121	119	2	122.51	−1.5
196	134	62	193	3
85	167	−82	104.5	−19.5
220	209	11	283	7.5
322	224	98	43.75	39
130				

Period 1 seasonal	3.5
Period 2 seasonal	59
Period 3 seasonal	−62.5

Table 15.1   Multiplicative and additive models

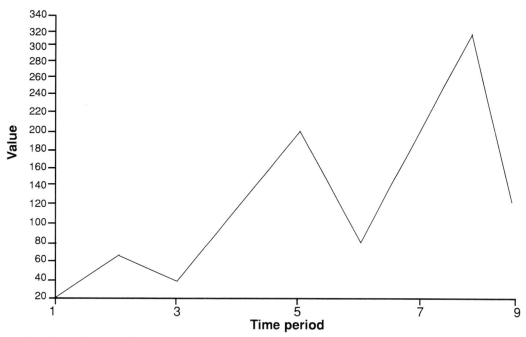

Fig. 15.1 Time series graph

2 (a) The graph is as shown in Fig. 15.2.

The most noticeable feature of the graph is the large peak in August each year, and a smaller but still evident peak in January. These are presuambly caused by the new registration letter and the new registration year respectively, and there are corresponding 'lows' in July and December as purchasers wait for the next month so as to buy a car with a more up-to-date registration letter or year. (Overseas students – and some British ones! – may well not be aware of this fact.) The trend appears to be slightly upwards.

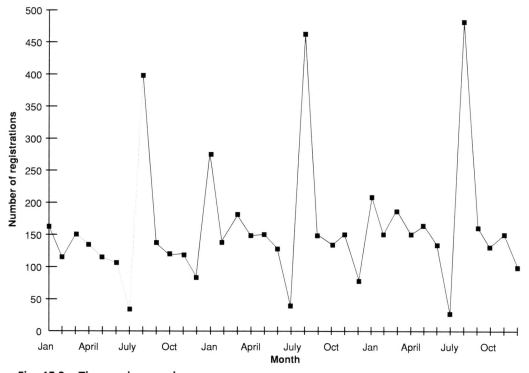

Fig. 15.2 Time series graph

(b) Since this is monthly data, a twelve-month moving average is needed to smooth it. The average will of course need centring.

(c) The full analysis of the series, with forecasts for January 1995 based on the assumption of a steady linear trend, is shown below. This analysis was produced using Excel.

(d) Neither model gives a very accurate result for January 1995 – the January seasonal figures are somewhat distorted by the very large peak in 1993, giving rise to oversetimates. Likewise neither method is very accurate in predicting the August behaviour of the series. There seems to be little to choose between the accuracy of the two methods, partly perhaps because the trend is pretty flat.

Month	Actual	12-Month MA	Centred MA	Additive seasonal	Additive forecast	Additive random	Mult seasonal	Mult forecast	Mult random
Jan	160								
February	118								
March	154								
April	144								
May	130								
June	111	141.08							
July	37	150.52	145.75	−108.75	30.74	6.26	25.39	36.26	102.03
August	392	151.67	151.04	240.96	417.90	−25.90	259.53	411.63	95.23
Sept	127	152.75	152.21	−25.21	130.13	−3.13	83.44	130.71	97.16
Oct	116	152.50	152.63	−36.63	121.18	−5.18	76.00	121.99	95.09
Nov	115	153.42	152.96	−37.96	120.86	−5.86	75.18	121.72	94.48
Dec	89	153.92	153.67	−64.67	79.45	9.55	57.92	82.09	108.41
Jan	272	154.08	154.00	118.00	233.65	38.35	176.62	232.47	117.00
February	133	159.00	156.54	−23.54	137.13	−4.13	84.96	137.66	96.62
March	167	160.17	159.58	7.42	175.65	−8.65	104.65	175.31	95.26
April	141	161.75	160.96	−19.96	142.24	−1.24	87.60	142.65	98.85
May	141	163.50	162.63	−21.63	146.65	−5.65	86.70	146.89	95.99
June	117	162.75	163.13	−46.13	126.20	−9.20	71.72	126.61	92.41
July	39	157.25	160.00	−121.00	44.99	−5.99	24.38	39.81	97.97
August	451	158.67	157.96	293.04	424.82	26.18	285.52	430.48	104.77
Sept	141	160.67	159.67	−18.67	137.59	3.41	88.31	137.11	102.84
Oct	135	161.33	161.00	−26.00	129.55	5.45	83.85	128.68	104.91
Nov	136	162.58	161.96	−25.96	129.86	6.14	83.97	128.88	105.52
Dec	80	164.42	163.50	−83.50	89.28	−9.28	48.93	87.35	91.59
Jan	206	164.42	164.42	41.58	244.07	−38.07	125.29	248.20	83.00
February	150	165.58	165.00	−15.00	145.59	4.41	90.91	145.09	103.38
March	191	186.42	166.00	25.00	182.07	8.93	115.06	182.36	104.74
April	149	166.00	166.21	−17.21	147.49	1.51	89.65	147.30	101.15
May	156	166.08	166.04	−10.04	150.07	5.93	93.95	149.98	104.01
June	139	166.83	166.46	−27.46	129.53	9.47	83.50	129.20	107.59
July	39		167.36						
August	465		168.26						
Sept	151		169.16						
Oct	130		170.06						
Nov	137		170.96						
Dec	89		171.86						
Jan			172.76		242.41			260.79	

Seasonals	Additive	Mult
Jan	79.65	150.9574
February	−19.41	87.93525
March	16.07	109.8539
April	−18.72	88.62342
May	−15.97	90.32743
June	−36.93	77.61426
July	−115.01	24.88047
August	266.86	272.5247
Sept	−22.07	85.87362
Oct	−31.45	79.9271
Nov	−32.10	79.57804
Dec	−74.22	53.42362

3 (a) The results, again generated by Excel, are shown below.

Week no.	Actual	Forecast alpha = 0.2	Error	Forecast alpha = 0.3	Error	Forecast alpha = 0.4	Error
1	27						
2	23	27	−4	27	−4	27	−4
3	23	26.20	−3.20	25.80	−2.80	25.40	−2.40
4	25	25.56	−0.56	24.96	−0.04	24.44	−0.56
5	26	25.45	0.55	24.97	1.03	24.66	1.34
6	29	25.56	3.44	25.28	3.72	25.20	3.80
7	25	26.25	−1.25	26.40	−1.40	26.72	−1.72
8	21	26.00	−5.00	25.98	−4.98	26.03	−5.03
9	22	25.00	−3.00	24.48	−2.48	24.02	−2.02
10	24	24.40	−0.40	23.74	0.26	23.21	0.79
	MSE		8.264118		7.966353		7.919865

(b) On the MSE criterion, alpha = 0.4 seems to be best. We cannot, of course, assume that this will be the best over the entire range of alpha values. With a spreadsheet it is quite easy to generate a full range from 0 to 1, and then plot a graph to try to determine the alpha giving minimum MSE. Students should, however, be encouraged not to use the MSE in a mechanistic way; in some situation (where forecasting too high has less serious consequences than forecasting too low, for instance, as might be the case in stock forecasting) other criteria may be more appropriate.

Chapter 16
FINANCIAL MATHEMATICS

Outline content

This chapter covers:
- compound interest and discounting calculations, and their application to problems involving annuities, hire purchase repayments, sinking funds, and investment appraisal.

Teaching this material

The content of this chapter does not relate to anything else in the book, and can very easily became a rather dry business of 'getting the right formula' to solve a particular problem. For this reason I have only given formulae for the fundamental compound interest and discounting situations, and have eschewed the formulae for annuities, etc., given in many texts. I think it is preferable that students think through more complex problems and relate them to these two basic processes.

Interest (no pun intended!) can be added to the topic by relating it to questions such as the true annual rate of interest charged by credit card companies – questions in which many students have a vested interest!

As regards computation, which can become quite heavy, I think it is important that students are encouraged to use their calculators in the most efficient way, making full use of constant multiplier facilities, etc. (*see* the Computational Note on p. 374 of *Quantitative Approaches in Business Studies*).

These computations are also ideally suited to spreadsheet calculation; actually constructing tables of discount factors, annuity factors, etc. using a spreadsheet can be a useful vehicle not only for enhancing understanding of the ideas of financial maths, but also for developing skill with TABLE and similar spreadsheet commands. Two examples are provided on the diskette: ANN.XLS performs annuity calculations, while SINK.XLS deals with sinking funds. The worksheets include lookup tables of the necessary factors, which could be extended by students to cover wider ranges of interest rates or time periods.

Solutions to the exercises

In examining solutions to all these problems, allowance should be made for the effect of rounding, which may produce discrepancies in the pence figures of the answers.

1 $1,000(1 + 0.15)^5 = £2,011.36$

2 After withdrawal of the first £200, £1,811.36 remains in the account. The interest on this in the next year is £271.70, which more than covers the next £200 withdrawn. Thus the total investment will continue to increase.

3 (a) $600(1 + 0.2)^3 = £1,036.80$

(b) Let the annual investment be $£x$.

Then the first $£x$ is invested for the full three years, and so amounts to $£x(1 + 0.15)$ by the time the machine is to be bought.

In a similar way we see that the total in the sinking fund by the time of the purchase is $x(1.15 + 1.15 + 1.15) = 3.99x$. This must be enough to cover the £1,036.80 inflated price of the item. So, $3.993375x = 1,036.80$, whence $x = £259.63$.

(This solution assumes that only three payments are made into the sinking fund – that is, there is no final payment made just before purchase of the item. This is not, of course, the only way of administering such a fund. It is also perhaps worth discussing the effect of rounding errors on this calculation – if the 3.993375 is rounded to 3.99, the answer differs by 22p.)

4 By the time the first payment is made, Fred owes, including interest, £525. After payment of the £100, the outstanding balance is £425. One month later, this has incurred interest raising it to £446.25. Continuing in this way, we find that six payments are enough to pay off the debt – the last payment being of £89.86. A common mistake here is to forget the last month's interest.

5 The easiest way to see what is going on here is to imagine that £100 is borrowed from each company for six months. Brackleycard will charge

$100(1 + 0.04)^6 = £126.53$, Excess £125, representing better value.

6 Suppose that $£x$ per year is withdrawn. The present value of the first withdrawal is $£x (1 + 0.15)^{-1}$. The PVs of the other five withdrawals may be found in the same way. The sum of all five is $3.353x$, which must be equal to the present value of the investment, namely £5,000. Thus $x = £1,491.20$.

7 The present value of the annuity is:

$500(1.1^{-3} + 1.1^{-4} + 1.1^{-5} + 1.1^{-6}) = $ approx. £1,309.50

8 The calculations are as follows:

Eskimo: purchase price = 150.00
Costs: $20 \times 1.15^{-1} = 17.39$
$20 \times 1.15^{-2} = 15.12$
$25 \times 1.15^{-3} = 16.44$
$40 \times 1.15^{-4} = 22.87$

Total PV of expenditure = 221.82
Less PV of second hand value = 28.59
Net cost = 193.23

Polar Bear: purchase price = 126.00 (with discount)
Costs: $25 \times 1.15^{-1} = 21.74$
$25 \times 1.15^{-2} = 18.90$
$25 \times 1.15^{-3} = 16.44$
$25 \times 1.15^{-4} = 14.29$
$5 \times 1.15^{-4} \; = 2.86$

Net cost = 200.23

So the Eskimo is a slightly cheaper buy.

9 The first machine gives revenues with a PV of £1,678.24 – less than the PV of the cost of the machine, indicating that it would be more profitable to leave the £1,700 in the bank. This means that the return on the investment represents a rate worse than 20 per cent.

The second machine gives revenues with a PV of £1,972.22 – again, less than the £2,000 outlay. If one other machine must be purchased, the first gives a slightly lower deficit; but neither represents a rate of return as good as 20 per cent.

Students do not always find it easy to understand just what a surplus or a deficit on the basis of NPV actually means. Using a spreadsheet it is quite easy by trial and error to arrive at an estimate of the Internal Rate of Return (the rate which, when used for discounting the project, gives neither a surplus nor a deficit), and this can give more insight into what is going on.

10 The computations are as shown below:

Date	Deposit	Withdrawal	Interest	Balance
Jan-01				11252.73
Jan-05		10.00		11242.73
Jan-09	4750.00			15992.73
Jan-15		5000.00		10992.73
Jan-28	2142.36			13135.09
Jan-31			52.54	13187.63
Feb-05		7.50		13180.13
Feb-12		500.00		12680.13
Feb-21	1413.47			14093.60
Feb-26		5000.00		9093.60
Feb-28			36.37	9129.97
Mar-01				9129.97

Suggestions for further work

It is helpful if some of the work of this chapter can be related to what students are covering in Accounting – with the aid of a spreadsheet more realistic projects with longer lives can be considered. Discussion of how a suitable discounting rate is arrived at can be interesting, while other possible areas of application are depreciation and the computation of insurance premiums (which relates this topic neatly with the probability and expected value material encountered earlier in the book).

Chapter 17
STOCK CONTROL

Outline content

This chapter covers:
- **the construction and solution of algebraic models for simple deterministic inventory problems.**

Teaching this material

I think the content of this chapter, not intrinsically exciting in itself, can best be motivated by using it as an example of the modelling (some would say the Operational Research) approach in practice. The actual mathematics involved is fairly simple, so that even less confident students should be able to see behind the algebraic details to the underlying philosophy of simplification/solution/verification. For those who find the abstraction of working with symbols for costs, demand, etc. too difficult, I would rely heavily on numerical examples. In particular, the logic of 'if annual demand is D items, and Q items are ordered at a time, then D/Q orders per annum will be required' seems to give many students problems. However, the question 'if we need 12,000 items a year, and we order 2,000 at a time, how many orders do we need?' is usually correctly answered, and the process used to arrive at the answer can then be generalised.

The worksheet INV.XLS contains the calculation of a table of costs similar to that on page 301. This can be particularly useful for experimenting with the sensitivity of solutions by introducing small changes to the order cost, demand, and so on; it could also be modified to cover the other situations included in this chapter (discounts, stock outs, making-and-using).

Solutions to the exercises

1. The stock-in-hand value should be 35, 47, 41, 34, 31, 22, 11, 46, 39, 32, 25, 20, 10, 23. This is simply a running total taking into account both deliveries and sales. The average weekly demand is then the total of the sales, 90 boxes, averaged over the two weeks – that is, 45 boxes per week.

2. The main point about plotting the graph is that it should be a step-function, *not* an attempt at a smooth curve.

3. There are two ways of approaching this question. One is to substitute into the EBQ formula on p. 385 of *Quantitative Approaches in Business Studies*:

   C = 50 pence, D = 45, and H = 5 pence per box per week, giving $q = \sqrt{2CD/H} = 30$ boxes per order – in other words, order three times per fortnight.

Alternatively, a table could be drawn up:

Order size	Number of orders/week	Order cost (p/week)	Average stock	Stock-holding cost (p/week)
45	1	50	22.5	112.5
15	3	150	7.5	37.5
30	1.5	75	15	75

The optimal policy is where order cost = stock-holding cost – that is, at order size 30, as before.

4 There are two policies to be compared here.

(a) Reduce order size to 20 boxes. This gives 45/20 = 2.25 orders per week, at a cost of $2.25 \times 50 = 112.5$ pence per week. Stock-holding cost is 10 (average stock) $\times 5 = 50$ pence per week. So total cost of this policy is 162.5 pence per week.

(b) Alternatively, continue to order 30 per week, but go out of stock by 10 so that capacity of 20 is never exceeded. This gives order cost of 75 pence as before.

Stock-holding cost is $5 \times 10 \times 2/3$ (because there is stock only for 2/3 of the cycle) = 33.3 pence per week.

Stock-out cost = $5 \times 5 \times 1/3 = 8.3$ pence per week. So total cost of this policy is 116.6 pence per week. It is, therefore, the cheaper policy.

5 With two days lead time on deliveries, at a minimum we should reorder when two days' supply remains, rather than waiting until stocks fall to zero. With a demand for 45 boxes a week, and assuming a 6-day week as indicated by the stock records, this would mean reordering when 15 boxes remain. This policy is sometimes implemented in practice by using a 'two-bin' system – the 15 boxes required during the lead time on orders would be put into a separate bin from the rest, so that when the main bin is empty, a reorder is triggered. Of course, it would be wise to maintain a buffer stock rather than working so close to the limit, especially given the random fluctuations in demand exhibited by the stockbook.

6 Here we have a 'make-and-use' situation. During the production phase, one-third of the items produced per day will be used, so the ratio of the 'make' section of the cycle to the 'use' section is 1:2. Thus the maximum stock held, given a total production of q items, will be 2q/3.

Stock-holding cost is thus based on half of this – that is, $£0.04 \times q/3$ per month.

In order to meet demand, 15000/q items must be made, giving a production cost of $£200 \times 15000/q$ per month.

As usual, costs will be minimised where these two elements are in balance:

$$0.04 \times q/3 = 200 \times 15000/q,$$

which solves to give q = 15,000. Thus each cycle should consist of one day of production followed by two days without production during which remaining stocks are used up.

The cost of this policy will be $0.04 \times 15000/3 + 200 \times 1 = £400$.

Suggestions for further work

There is scope for discussing the sensitivity question further, either numerically or symbolically if students have the capability. For those with a knowledge of calculus (partial derivatives) the question of stock-outs can be pursued in more generality than the simple comparison of the two policies outlined here.

If your syllabus will include some simulation later (*see* Chapter 19), it might be as well at this stage to have a brief discussion of the effect of variable demand on the problem. This can be taken up again when simulation has been covered. It is also possible to link the variable demand idea back to the concept of expected value encountered in Chapter 8 – in fact, the 'tea stall' example in that chapter involved working out the expected demand, given an empirical demand distribution.

Chapter 18
LINEAR PROGRAMMING

Outline content

This chapter covers:
- **the formulation and solution of linear programming problems in two variables by graphical means;**
- **the investigation of the sensitivity of the solution to changes in the constraints and in the objective function coefficients.**

Teaching this material

Students often choose to answer problems on linear programming in examinations, since they are easily recognised, and there is a fairly standard routine for tackling the problem and arriving at a solution. In my experience, the part they find difficult is what goes around the outside of the solution process – namely, on the one hand the formulation from the original verbally-expressed problem, and on the other the interpretation of the solution in practical terms. This is the part, therefore, which needs emphasising in teaching the topic.

It may be questioned whether, now that there are many good computer packages for linear programming which will cope with problems with many variables just as easily as two, there is any point in concentrating on two-variable problems and graphical solutions. I believe there is, certainly for students for whom it is not appropriate to get involved with linear algebra, duality, etc. Having seen the 'nuts and bolts' of the graphical solution, and particularly, having seen how the sensitivity analysis can be related to moving lines around on the graph, prevents the procedures of a package from simply becoming a 'black box', and aids the student in interpreting the output from more complex problems. The kind of algorithm used in such packages can be explained to these students in terms of 'searching through' the vertices of the feasible region for an optimal solution, in much the same way as is done by hand.

Solutions to the exercises

1   Let B represent the number of cabbages grown, and F the number of cauliflowers. Then the formulation is:

Planting time:	$2B + 3F \leq 120$
Space:	$B + 2F \leq 72$
Cooking:	$B \leq 36$
Minimum cauliflowers:	$F \geq 10$

Maximise $4B + 3F$

(a) (*See* Fig. 18.1) Optimal solution is B = 36, F = 16, giving 192 helpings.

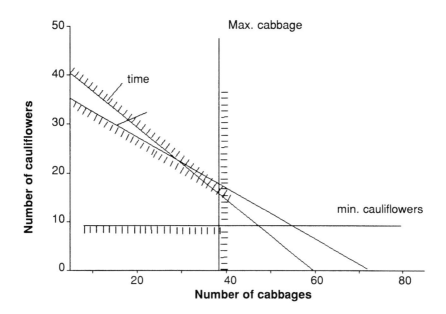

Fig. 18.1 Linear programming graph for cabbages/cauliflowers

(b) Yes – the number of helpings from a cauliflower can increase to six without altering the optimal solution (as long as the number from a cabbage remains the same). This is because the slope of the objective function line must remain between that of the 'maximum cabbage' constraint and the 'planting time' constraint, as seen from the graph.

(c) If the first constraint becomes 2B + 3F ≤ 105, while the other tight constraint, 'cooking', remains at B ≤ 36, then the new optimal solution is F = 11, B = 36, giving 177 helpings.

2 Let the numbers of Silver Shadows and Princesses be S and P respectively. The formulation is then:

Total number of guests:	6S + 4P ≥ 36
Total hire requirement:	S + P ≥ 7
Car park:	S + P ≤ 12
Joneses:	S ≥ 2

Minimise 10S + 9P

(a) (*See* Fig.18.2) Minimum cost is achieved with 4 Shadows and 3 Princesses at a total cost of £67.

(b) If the number of guests increases by one, the first constraint becomes:

6S + 4P ≥ 37

The other tight constraint at the solution point is the total hire requirement:

S + P ≥ 7

Solving these simultaneously gives S = 4.5, P = 2.5, at a cost of £67.50, so the extra cost is only 50p. This applies in the range 32 to 42 guests, as can be seen by moving the total guest constraint line on the graph.

(c) The slope of the objective function line has to remain between the slopes of the total guest constraint and the total hire constraint, if the optimal solution is to remain valid. This leads to 2/3 < Cost of Princess/Cost of Shadow < 1.

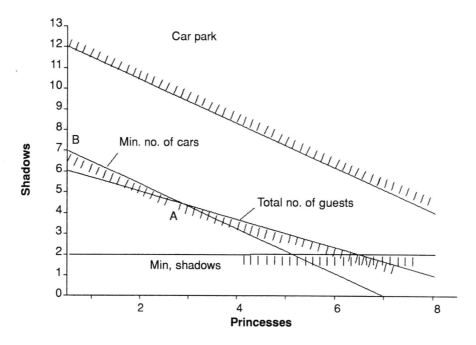

Fig. 18.2 Linear programming graph for cars problem

3 In this case the objective is to maximise S + P, so the objective function line is parallel to the 'minimum number of cars' constraint. Thus, instead of just one solution point, we have a whole set of solutions – namely, all integer points on the line AB on the graph.

4 The method of 'moving the objective line in (or out)' to find the optimum cannot be guaranteed to work when there are nonlinear constraints.

6 The formulation is the point of this question – as there is only one constraint, the actual solution can be seen quite easily even though there are three variables. Defining the variables as:

P = number of pounds of Puce Label produced per week
V = number of pounds of Olive Label produced per week
T = number of pounds of Teabags produced per week

we can say that the total amount of China tea used is:

$2P/9 + V/9 + T/10$

And similarly for the other two types of tea. The cost constraint thus becomes:

$1.2(2P/9 + V/9 + T/10) + 0.8(4P/9 + 2V/3 + T/2) + 1.0(P/3 + 2V/9 + 2T/5) \le 480$

which simplifies to $0.96P + 0.89V + 0.92T \le 480$.

To work out the profit on each type of product, we need the cost of production. Cost of producing a pound of Puce Label is 0.96, as found above, so profit on P will be $(1.44 - 0.96) \times P = 0.48P$. Similarly for the two other products. Thus, the objective is to maximise:

$$0.48P + 0.31V + 0.36T$$

It is not too difficult to visualise that in three dimensions the constraint represents a plane, and that the vertices of the feasible region will be given by substituting $V = T = 0$, $P = T = 0$, $P = V = 0$ into the constraint equation. This gives $P = 502.33$, $V = 540$, $T = 521.74$ as the non-zero co-ordinates at the vertices, revealing that the maximum profit will be when 502.33 pounds of Puce Label per week are produced – the profit here being £243.13 – and 111.63 lb of China, 223.26 lb of Indian and 167.44 lb of Ceylon tea are used per week.

Suggestions for further work

There is not much mileage in going further with purely graphical LP work. With the aid of a good package, the emphasis can shift to formulation and interpretation – both of which students find more difficult than grinding through a simplex algorithm. However, I believe that having seen a graphical approach is useful in interpreting the results of a package – it helps prevent a purely mechanical interpretation in which the students simply memorise the position in a printout of the scarcity value of the variable 1, and so on.

Chapter 19
NETWORK ANALYSIS

Outline content

This chapter covers:
- **the construction of networks for project planning by both activity-on-arrow and activity-on-node methods;**
- **the use of the network to determine the critical activities and the shortest time for the job;**
- **the construction of Gantt charts and their use in manpower planning and smoothing.**

Teaching this material

Network analysis has the advantage of being a very obviously 'useful' topic, and one which students with work experience are quite likely to have come across being used in practice. However, it also has the drawback – from the student's point of view – that there is no 'standard' method for the construction of a network. Each case must be thought through from first principles, and with a complex problem it is unlikely that the first attempt at drawing the network will turn out to be correct.

There are, of course, general guidelines which can be borne in mind: the fact that there should be only one starting and finishing point for the network, and each activity should appear only once – a point which is sometimes overlooked by newcomers to the subject. I have deliberately eschewed, however, the use of the many formulae for earliest and latest times, floats, etc. given in some OR texts – at this elementary level it seems to me that they are more confusing than helpful.

Though the book contains some mention of the activity-on-node format for the network, the major emphasis is still on activity-on-arrow. This is because some external examining bodies still require this version, and for students of those bodies the difficulties of logical dummies need a good deal of attention. The activity-on-node format being a good deal easier, no-one who has grasped activity-on-arrow should have difficulty in switching. There is also the question of which format the software to which the reader has access (if any) assumes.

Solutions to the exercises

1 No increase in project duration is required if this is the case. A possible Gantt chart is then as shown in Fig.19.1.

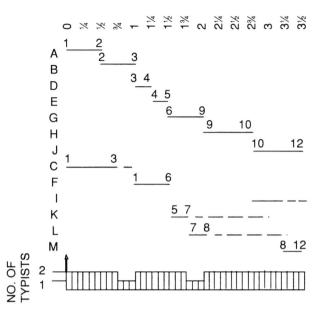

Fig. 19.1   Gantt chart for practical exercise 1

2 With the current availability of staff, no delay in project completion is required, if the senior partner is willing to drink his coffee while checking the typing (see Fig. 19.2).

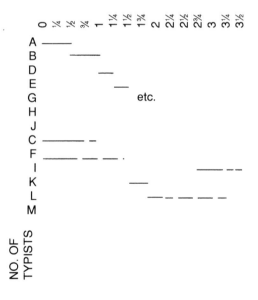

Fig. 19.2   Gantt chart for practical exercise 2

3 The reduction of activity H by 15 minutes will not change the critical path, but will reduce the overall project time by 15 minutes.

4 (a)   The network is shown in Fig.19.3, in activity on arrow format. There are two critical paths ADEGHJ and ADFGHJ, both of which have length 12.5 minutes, so the claimed time of 10 minutes cannot be met.

   (b)   The Gantt chart in Fig.19.4 indicates that 13.5 minutes will be the minimum time for the process if only two staff are available.

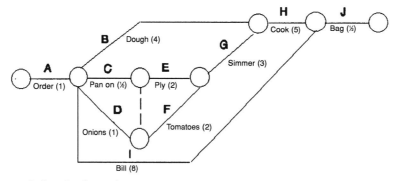

Fig. 19.3   A network for the fast pizza process

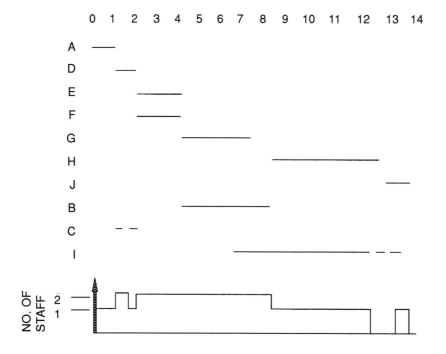

Fig. 19.4   Gantt chart for practical exercise 4(b)

5 (a) The status of the activity 'watching for Customs and Excise' in this network needs a little discussion. As it is an activity which takes place in parallel with 'brewing' and 'bottling', its duration is exactly as long as theirs. Rather than including it as a separate activity in the network, therefore, it is preferable to think of it in combination with these two activities, and simply remember when drawing up the Gantt chart that an extra person is required to watch during this phase of the project. That being so, the network could be drawn as shown in Fig.19.5, giving critical activities ADCFH, and shortest project time 19.5 days.

  (b) The question does not actually state the number of people required for each activity, but if it is assumed that one person per activity is adequate, then the project can be completed with only two people available in a variety of ways. One possibility is shown in the Gantt chart in Fig.19.6.

6 (a) The network is as shown in Fig.19.7. Of course the labels 1 and 2 are purely arbitrary here.

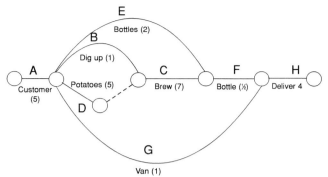

Fig. 19.5 A network illustrating the solution to practical exercise 5(g)

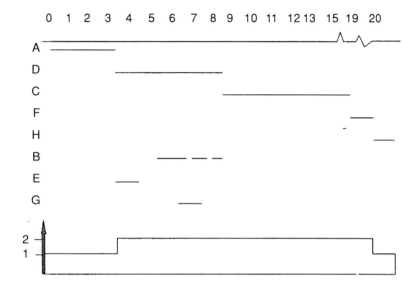

Fig. 19.6 Gantt chart giving one possible way of completing the project

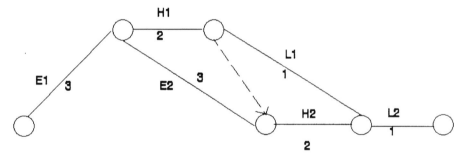

Fig. 19.7 Network for practical exercise 6(a)

(b) The critical path is El–E2–H2–L2, with a time of nine weeks. There is no need to draw a Gantt chart to answer this part of the question – it can be worked out as follows:

Excavation gang – on site for 9 weeks, of which 6 are working, at a cost of 6 × 800 + 3 × 400 = £6,000.
Hardcore gang – 4 × 800 + 5 × 400 = £5,200.
Top surface gang – 2 × 800 + 7 × 400 = £4,400.
Total cost = £15,600.

7 The activities mentioned in the scenario can be listed as follows:

A	Roof repairs	4 weeks preceded by –
B	Structural alterations	3 weeks preceded by A
C	Plumbing	2 weeks preceded by A
D	Gas	1 week preceded by A
E	Decorations	2 weeks preceded by B
F	Cloakrooms	1 week preceded by C
G	Catering area	6 weeks preceded by C, D
H	Landscaping	8 weeks preceded by A
I	Furnishing and carpets	2 weeks preceded by E,F,G,H

Without any of the complications being taken into account, the network is as shown in Fig.19.8. This gives a time of 14 weeks for the project so, as it stands, the 12 weeks target cannot be met. If the Gas Board restriction means that D must be preceded by C, this will extend the project duration by one week. The delay to the decoration of the conference room will not extend the project duration, since there are three weeks' float on E, which could start in week 7, but need not start until week 10.

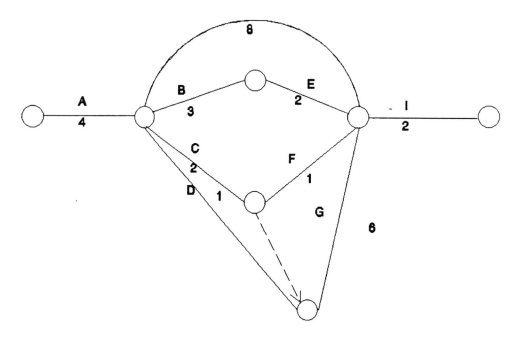

Fig. 19.8   A network for the case study question

There are actually two critical paths in the network as drawn – ACGI and AHI. The most promising line of attack, if the project duration is to be reduced to 12 weeks, would seem to be allowing the landscaping to continue in parallel with the furnishing and carpets (activity I). This seems realistic, and could meet the 12-week target.

Suggestions for further work

Although getting students to construct networks for projects they are familiar with – such as changing the wheel of a car, or making a cup of tea – can be entertaining, there is a great deal of scope for argument both in the breaking down of the project into activities, and in the sequencing of these activities.

Network analysis can be linked with probability by considering what happens if, instead of a fixed duration for each activity, we allow a distribution of activity times. With normally distributed times, working out the overall duration only requires a knowledge of the fact that variance of the sum = sum of the variances. However, the more usual approach is to use the 'optimistic/pessimistic/most likely' approach, which requires a knowledge of non-normal continuous distributions.

Another interesting line to pursue is the question of the 'crashing' of activities – paying a certain sum in order to reduce the duration of an activity (by employing additional labour, for example). Clearly the best strategy is to crash the cheapest activity on the critical path first, by the largest amount possible. This may well change the critical path, and the process can become quite complex with a large network.

Chapter 20
SIMULATION

Outline content

This chapter covers:
- **the concept of using simulation via random number distributions to reflect the behaviour of a stochastic system;**
- **the mechanics of carrying out a simulation for a queuing problem.**

Teaching this material

Simulation, at the simple level at which it is covered in this chapter, is another technique which students often find tricky – not because of any technical complexity, but because there is no 'standard method' for the layout of a simulation. I think the first essential is to ensure that students grasp the underlying concept of simulation – the idea of using a distribution of random numbers to mirror the unpredictable behaviour of a stochastic system.

This is harder than it sounds. Many readers on first encountering the idea have difficulty reconciling the long-term predictability reflected in, say, a frequency distribution of arrival times, with the short-term unpredictability which makes it impossible to say when the next customer will arrive. Using a more familiar device, such as a die or a roulette spinner, rather than simply a table of random numbers to begin with, may help to crystallise the ideas. Most people can accept that with a fair spinner of 22 divisions, in the long run each number should come up on 1/22nd of occasions, but to predict which number will come up on the next spin is impossible (unless you believe in 'a system'!). From this the step can be made to a spinner with divisions of unequal sizes, representing a non-uniform distribution, and hence to a distribution of random numbers.

Understanding of this topic is immeasurably enhanced by the use of a suitable computer package. I say 'suitable' because some of the commercial simulation packages and languages available are definitely not suited to teaching use – the overheads of learning the system are too great, and the 'can't see the wood for the trees' syndrome sets in. But a package which enables students to see the effect of alterations to the parameters of a problem, such as an increase in the number of service points available, or a change in queuing discipline, can provide experiential learning with far less effort than the carrying out of hand simulations. A simulation written by the teacher, which allows students to experiment by varying parameters, can also be useful.

It is for this reason that I have provided the worksheet SIM.WK1 on the diskette. This is a single-queue, two-server simulation which uses empirical distributions to specify lookup tables within Excel. The distributions can be altered, though it needs to be understood that they are specified in the form of 'strictly less than' cumulative tables.

Thus, for example, suppose we have the table shown:

Cum prob	0.0	0.2	0.5	0.8	0.9	1	
Inter-arrival time	1	2	3	4	5	6	mins

Then if we wish to generate an inter-arrival time corresponding to the number 0.7342 obtained using the Excel command (i.e. from the uniform distribution on [0,1]), we scan the top row of the table until we find a figure greater than 0.7342 – in this case, 0.8. The figure of 3 minutes below this indicates that 80 per cent of values are strictly less than 3 minutes, so the random number 0.7342 yields a time of 2 minutes.

The worksheet simulates 20 arrivals, though rows could be inserted to extend this. To generate a new random sample of arrivals, the macro \a needs to be invoked by holding down ALT while pressing A; this macro generates 20 random numbers into each of columns A and B, then fixes their values so that the worksheet is accordingly updated. Information on average waiting time and average idle time of the service channels is provided, though of course one will not always require both these figures.

Rather more on-screen instructions are provided with this worksheet than is the case with the others on the diskette, so that students have full details of how to use it without being given further written information.

Solutions to the exercises

1 The distribution is:

01–06
07–17
18–35
36–60
61–81
82–95
96–00

2 The distribution for interview times is:

8 minutes 01–08	11 minutes 46–75
9 minutes 09–22	12 minutes 76–93
10 minutes 23–45	13 minutes 94–00

For arrivals the distribution is:

2 mins early 01–12	1 min late 73–88
1 min early 13–32	2 mins late 89–00
On time 33–72	

(This could be arranged in other ways.)

While it is not possible to give an 'answer' for a simulation, it can be instructive to get students to compare their solutions, and see how much variation arises with the use of different groups of random numbers.

3 This simulation might be tracked by using headings very similar to those used in the chapter for the computer terminals simulation, replacing 'terminal' by 'repair worker'. A discussion could follow on the relative costs of 'worker idle' versus 'job kept waiting'. It is interesting to speculate on the strategies operated by various

organisations in this field – for example, it is clear that many hospital outpatient departments view doctors' time as far more valuable than that of patients, and therefore run their appointment system on the basis of minimising doctors' waiting time, even at the expense of maximising the patients'!

4 This is best tackled by students working in groups, since gathering sufficient data to get a reasonable idea of distributions of waiting/arrival times can be time-consuming. The kind of 'single-queue, multiple-server' discipline now used in many large banks and post offices makes a particularly interesting study. Some discussion of seasonal (daily, weekly, etc.) fluctuations in the arrival and service-time patterns should be encouraged.

Suggestions for further work

The material of this chapter has concentrated on queuing simulations, but the ideas can be linked back to Chapter 17 on Inventory, and simulation of unpredictable demand contrasted with the deterministic approach to stock control given in that chapter.